BLACK WOMEN'S LIVES

BLACK WOMEN'S LIVES

stories of power and pain

KRISTAL BRENT ZOOK

NATION
BOOKS

BLACK WOMEN'S LIVES
STORIES OF POWER AND PAIN

Published by
Nation Books
An Imprint of Avalon Publishing Group Inc.
245 West 17th Street, 11th Floor
New York, NY 10011

AVALON
publishing group incorporated

Library of Congress Cataloging-in-Publication Data is available.

ISBN: 1-56025-790-3
ISBN 13: 978-1-56025-790-5

9 8 7 6 5 4 3 2 1

Book design by Maria Elias
Printed in the United States of America
Distributed by Publishers Group West

For the women, and those who love them.

CONTENTS

ACKNOWLEDGMENTS

My deepest thanks go to the following individuals and institutions for their support and guidance:

Reverend Jesse L. Jackson, Sr. who first suggested that I travel south to talk with working women in the catfish and poultry plants. Thank you for inspiring me to speak so many truths, as I see them. The Alicia Patterson Foundation, for providing generous financial support and making this book possible. Nation Books and Ruth Baldwin for seeing the vision clearly. *Essence* magazine and Susan Taylor, thank you for providing a space for us all to breathe and grow. Students and faculty at the Graduate School of Journalism at Columbia University. Eugene Robinson of *The Washington Post,* a constant supporter.

Sarah White, you are a precious and kindred spirit; Rosalie and Clifford Williams, Sakia Gunn, Valencia and Gail Bailey, Lynn Battle, Yvonne Sanders-Butler, Floyd Butler, and the Browns Mill Elementary Arts and Magnet School staff, Gina Prince-Bythewood and Reggie Bythewood, Candace and

Bruce Matthews, the families of Kenitha Saafir and Kristin High, and especially Reverend Patricia Strong-Fargas and Holman Arthurs, Richard and Hilliard Jimerson and the residents and staff at North Rehabilitation Facility.

My dearest friends, for listening and cheering me on.

And most of all, I thank my family who loved and nurtured me long before I ever put pen to page, and in doing so made my path that much clearer.

PREFACE

I am privileged to be a journalist. In writing about black women's lives over the past decade, I have been given the honor of recording stories that would have otherwise remained untold. The women featured in this book were followed mostly through instinct. I was compelled by those whose experiences struck me as being richly layered and complex. I could not have written about them, however, if they had not allowed me into their lives and given me their trust.

This journey began in 1995, when I went to Mississippi to speak to black women working in catfish and poultry plants. I didn't know exactly what I was looking for. Only that the lives of these women were so different from my own. It was only a few generations earlier that their families and my own had shared a common way of life and culture, and yet it seemed as though we now lived on different planets. I went South because, as a biracial woman who was raised by two generations of African American women in an urban environment, I needed to understand the chasm between myself and those who remained in the rural fields that my grandmother had left behind as a young girl. I needed to look back for myself, even if she did not care to.

I went South because there was no longer a black newspaper like *The Chicago Defender* from the North, being secretly dropped by Pullman porters off the backs of trains to maintain our links between past and present. I went because I could not create a conversation out of space and distance. Over the next decade, I would return to the southern states, where 55 percent of the African American population currently lives, nearly three dozen times. I would also travel to the northeast and northwest, visiting with women from all walks of life. My only regret is that the center of the country is not well-represented in this collection. Ultimately, I suppose this book is more about common ground than geography.

The portraits presented here are, at their core, investigations into the survival and health of African American communities. They are stories about weight and obesity; toxic chemicals in our homes and environments; ambition and economic striving; self esteem; multiracial identity; cultural estrangement and assimilation; AIDS unions and organized labor; food; trust; anger and corporate greed; cognitive and emotional disabilities, learning and education; homosexuality; marriage; hate crimes; faith; sisterhood; friendship; death; addiction; and all manner of violence.

There are many women whose stories I would have liked to

tell but simply was not able. Lateefah Simon, for one, is a young woman who never finished college, lived in the projects, worked at Taco Bell, and had a baby at the age of nineteen. She became executive director of San Francisco's Center for Young Women's Development, which employs low-income women who are trapped in the juvenile justice system. For her work, Lateefah, now twenty-seven, was awarded a "genius grant" from the MacArthur Foundation: $500,000 to do with as she pleases.

I was touched by the story of Bonnie Hughey, an accountant in Southfield, Michigan, who made the decision to change her life. Bonnie once weighed 450 pounds and could barely lift herself out of a car. At thirty-one, she moved out of her mother's home, joined Weight Watchers, and lost half her weight: 225 pounds. At thirty-three, she went on her first date ever. Lunch with a Web site designer. Bonnie will remain in my thoughts as she struggles to confront her painful past and to look toward a more hopeful future.

I would have been proud to include Cassandra Burton and Faye Williams of the non-profit Sisterspace and Books in Washington, D.C., the only African American woman-owned bookstore in the country to specialize in books about black women. Cassandra and Faye have provided an oasis and safe space for so many in their community. They epitomize the true meaning of loving sisterhood.

And I would have been honored to offer up an intimate portrait of someone I admire deeply: Congresswoman Barbara Lee, whom I followed in an elevator (with my other hero Maxine Waters) and was able to interview for approximately seven minutes as we walked the halls of Congress. Not nearly enough for a chapter in a book, unfortunately.

For reasons that are not entirely clear to me, a relatively large number of women featured here are in long-term healthy marriages and partnerships. Perhaps I was drawn to their stories, consciously or unconsciously, because so many African American women do not, in fact, have such partnerships. In fact, about 54 percent of African American women between the ages of twenty-four and thirty-four have never been married, compared to 35 percent for other Americans. And black women are more likely to be divorced or separated than the general population: two out of three such marriages end in divorce, compared to one in two for non-African American women. This leaves the vast majority of black women in the category of alone. The wives featured in this book, therefore, are not typical, but perhaps their stories can offer some insight into why that is so.

My personal growth and ongoing journey of empowerment has been interwoven deeply with those of the women who have allowed me into their homes and hearts over the past ten years. They have been conduits, vessels, and messengers, on a profoundly spiritual level. And, yet, I believe that their collective impact will be somehow far greater than any one interaction would have been alone. This book, therefore, is a meditation on the sum of our parts.

1.

Gina Prince-Bythewood with her sons, Cassius and Toussaint.

ARTIST
Woodland Hills, California

I found filmmaker Gina Prince-Bythewood in the sweltering Nevada desert on an August morning last summer, waiting for a television sitcom shoot to begin at the Little White Wedding Chapel in downtown Las Vegas. It was the part of town where drive-through wedding chapels are found in high density, sometimes two and three to a city block. This location, a fixture for half a century, was right in the thick of the matrimonial action with its plastic rose garden, Astroturf gazebo, and hurried "I do's." But instead of white limousines, there were actors' trailers and craft services trucks filling the driveway on this day, as crew members ambled about carrying zeppelins, black-and-white screens, metal C-stands, lamps, and lights. A boom operator took a bite of white powder donut and flashed a smile at this visiting reporter, while someone offered the director of photography a Red Bull.

Gina stood like an athlete on the basketball court, legs firmly rooted and forming an upside down "V." With light brown skin and long, curly hair pulled back into a ponytail, she was consummately casual, wearing Nike sneakers, a vintage Dr Pepper T-shirt, and a green "Save Darfur" wristband to stop the genocide in the Sudan. I watched as she surveyed the actors in the scene: first adjusting her khakis by yanking them up quickly, like a guy might do; then, folding her arms and lowering her head slightly, studying the scene like a coach willing a final point.

Something of a "contradiction" even by her own estimation, Gina is both socially uncomfortable and professionally confident. Sometimes the contradictions collide. In fact she is so "fiercely reserved" as one friend puts it, that the young writer blew her first big job interview by muttering shy, monosyllabic answers to a roomful of television producers. Even today, being the first to arrive at a restaurant puts her on edge, and meeting strangers remains difficult. "I sometimes have trouble looking them in the eye," she confesses. And yet put her on a set, say her friends and colleagues, and she is clearly in command. She is both extraordinarily certain of her own abilities and vision, and at the same time, uncomfortable, as she puts it, "in her own skin."

Among filmmakers there are some major (and often insurmountable) differences of form and style between theatrical film and television. These differences have to do with multiple versus single-camera shoots, for example; stiff steady cams as opposed to the jostled unpredictability of hand-held; three-walled sets as opposed to the freedom of no walls; and constrained six-second mood shots as opposed to the luxury of fifteen. For these reasons and others, Gina, like most filmmakers, would rather be on a movie set than a television sitcom. But then again, this wasn't just any sitcom.

This was the 2005 season premiere episode of *Girlfriends*, the hit UPN series created by Gina's close friend Mara Brock Akil, who sat in a nearby director's chair wearing loose khaki shorts, black tank top, and Birkenstock-style sandals. Because of her shyness, one senses that Gina would be perfectly happy to let Mara—who chats away vivaciously—take over the interview and answer questions for her. It could be done, she implies. After all, says Gina, indicating with her finger the small space between Mara's shoulder and her own, "there's a lot of history here."

✳ ✳ ✳

That history began more than eleven years ago, in 1994, when Gina was a story editor and Mara was a writer's trainee on the Fox series *South Central*. Gina, then in her early twenties, was also a young director who already had a CBS Schoolbreak Special under her belt. *What About Your Friends?* (a movie that could have been easily been dubbed a teenage *Girlfriends*) followed three high school graduates preparing to start their first year at the historically black Spelman College in Atlanta, Georgia. It was no small beginning for a career. The film won an NAACP Image Award for Best Children's Special, plus Emmy nominations for Best Writing and Best Directing.

Following the phenomenal success of NBC's *The Cosby Show*—which ran for eight years and was the number one show in primetime from 1985 to 1989—the young writer made her first entry into the television industry with Bill Cosby's spin-off sitcom NBC's *A Different World*, a series about black college life. Under Cosby's watchful eye, the show was given a great deal of freedom (although some would maintain, not nearly enough) to explore issues of race, gender, and economic disparity. Cosby, who met Gina as a young athlete and aspiring film student at a USC-UCLA track meet, took a personal interest and assisted her with internships and networking in the entertainment industry.

In 1991, just after her graduation from college, Gina was made an apprentice writer on *A Different World*, which was executive produced by Susan Fales-Hill and directed by Debbie Allen. As Gina acknowledges gratefully, it was "a show that was essentially run by black women." While at *A Different World*, Gina met Reggie Rock Bythewood, a playwright from the Bronx who had come to Hollywood as an early recipient of the prestigious Disney's Writers Fellowship Program. Reggie and Gina, who would later marry, shared an interest in bringing relevant social issues into their scripts, with Reggie penning an especially memorable episode of *A Different World* that dealt with domestic violence. "The cast was always excited by Reggie's writing," recalls Gina, "because he always had something political to say."

After *A Different World*, Reggie went on to become supervising producer on the Fox drama *New York Undercover*, which launched in 1994 as the first dramatic series ever to star both African American and Latino leads. As I noted in my 1999 book, *Color by Fox: The Fox Network and the Revolution in Black Television*, the writing staff on the show was unique in that it employed nearly all people of color. The series tackled difficult social issues such as the burning of black churches, health care in Harlem, and the Puerto Rican movement for national independence.

In 1994, Gina landed at *South Central*, another exceptional series with a largely black production team. It too defied the sitcom genre by infusing it with drama and difficult storylines about gang violence, unemployment, single motherhood, and tensions between Latinos and African Americans in the inner city.

But the world of black television production shifted dramatically in 1994 when the Fox network cancelled the majority of its African American-produced shows, including *South Central*. Shows like *Roc*, starring Charles Dutton, and *The Sinbad Show*, starring the comedian Sinbad, were taken off the schedule for reasons that remain, as I argue in *Color by Fox*, largely unclear. Many of these shows were successful with their target "urban" demographic. And yet, as industry insiders argued, the network hoped to move out of "ghettoized" African American and Latino programming, and to court the young white male demographic that it now deemed more profitable.

In the post-1994 television universe, Gina found herself thrust onto relatively unfamiliar terrain: an industry in which all-black writing staffs were the exception rather than the rule. In 1994, she was hired on *Sweet Justice*, an NBC hour-long drama starring Cicely Tyson as an attorney in a civil rights law firm. There were no other African American attorneys in this fictional firm, nor were there any black writers on staff. When Gina was brought onboard, she helped to bring in actor Cree Summers to help diversify the cast. But her troubles on the set began when producers canned a script that was close to her heart. It was about a white family that wanted to adopt a black child. Gina, herself adopted by a white family, had written the script based on her own experiences. In it, she had voiced some of her opinions through the character of a social worker who argued that black children should be placed in black homes. The show's producers rejected the episode as "too black." "That killed me," recalls Gina. "Just killed me."

* * *

Born in Chicago, Illinois, on June 10, 1969, to a Caucasian mother and an African American father, Gina was placed in foster care and adopted at the age of three weeks by Robert Prince, a computer programmer of Irish descent, and Maria Prince, a nurse who was born in El Salvador to a German father and Salvadoran mother. The couple's first son, Jeffrey, had been born in 1963 with spina bifida and lived just six hours. The Princes had looked into an adoption program at that time, but decided against it after questioning whether or not they were simply trying to "replace their lost child," as Robert Prince put it to me, speaking by phone from his home in Northern California.

In 1965, Maria gave birth to a daughter named Tatia. The couple's second daughter, Crista, followed in 1967. Still intent on having a full house, the Princes decided that now was the right time to adopt. And so, in 1969, when Maria was four months pregnant again, they decided to adopt Gina. In 1971, the Princes also adopted Josh, who was seventeen months old at the time, and like Gina, also biracial.

Why adopt mixed race children? I asked Robert Prince.

"We felt like white kids will get adopted by *someone* and so we should try to adopt children who would have more difficulty getting placed," he explained. His tone was humble, as though he himself were searching for the right answer. "Maybe we might have hesitated to adopt a totally black child," he added, "because . . . I don't know, that just seemed like too big of a leap."

Theirs was a wholesome lifestyle in the white suburban community of Pacific Grove, about two hours south of San Francisco. And for the Princes, it was important that their children be involved in a wide variety of sports and recreational activities: soccer, softball, basketball. Today, Gina credits sports with keeping her away from drugs and alcohol. Her response to peer pressure was simple: "I'm an athlete." It worked, she says. "My dad came to every game and cheered real loud."

And the Princes were strict. None of their children were allowed to watch R-rated movies before age seventeen and early curfews were enforced. When the family television died (Gina was twelve), Bob and Maria simply decided to do without it. "I can remember as a child going to bed at like

7:00 or 8:00 P.M.," recalls Gina, "when it was still light out-side! But in retrospect I think it was a good thing." The simple values she was raised with are apparent even today. If you ask her favorite foods Gina will tell you turkey bacon, pizza, lasagna, enchiladas. Girl-next-door food. Her passions are equally unpretentious. She wants to raise good kids. Make good movies. Play sports. Watch Laker games. She is nothing if not down-to-earth.

But as a young adult, Gina began to wrestle with her anger about being placed in an all-white environment without the tools that she needed to understand racism. One memory that haunts her still is the time she was in an art class and some kids tacked a sketch on the wall: it was a black man hanging from a noose. Her teacher did nothing. On another occasion, she found the letters "KKK" scratched into her wooden school desk. As a teenager, she remembers sitting alone and crying for hours at a school dance while her white girlfriends sashayed the night away. "There were only two black boys in the entire school," she says, "and one was my brother."

"I can still remember the first time Gina was called a nigger," says Bob Prince, his voice breaking with emotion. "She was only about eight years old." The slur was made by a boy on her soccer team. "She didn't understand what was happening. I tried to explain, but what do you say?"

So what did he say?

"That there are bad people in the world and you just have to ignore them."

Gina's family didn't talk much about race when she was a young girl. "They just told me that I should act like it doesn't bother me and to ignore it. But when you have to act like it doesn't bother you," she adds, "it kind of kills your spirit." Gina's close friend Felicia Henderson (creator and executive producer of the Showtime dramatic series *Soul Food*) calls Robert Prince "a decent human being without a racist bone in his body." And yes, she adds, it was probably deeply emotional for him to experience those incidents. "But the difference is that Gina wasn't raised with someone who could give historical perspective to those emotions."

At fourteen, Gina went away to basketball camp in San José, California, where she first realized that she was different from other African American kids. She didn't fit in. Nor did she fit in at home, in the all-white community of Pacific Grove. To escape the pain of isolation she became a self-described soap opera junkie (once her family had a television again), and even watched some episodes *twice a day*. In the midst of both "an identity crisis and a family crisis," she says, television was her way to "sit and escape and not think." She felt alone in the world. And in many ways, she was.

As children, Gina and her brother Josh were best friends— hiking and camping in the Santa Cruz mountains near their home and picking huckleberries that their mother would use to garnish pancakes. Josh always had trouble in school, recalls Bob Prince, "difficulty reading and comprehending." There was frustration and anger because of this, and their son had a temper. But at the time, no one could have known the true extent of his illness. For Josh, racial discrimination didn't seem to be the problem. Unlike Gina, he had never been one to concern himself much with the prejudices of others. At age twenty-four, he was diagnosed with bipolar disorder.

Looking back, Gina now realizes that Josh had been "self-medicating," as a teenager, with acid and marijuana in an effort to cope with his wild mood swings, anger, and depression. One night he had an especially bad acid trip. There was an argument that became physical as he tried to push past his father to leave the house. Josh ended up leaving home at age fifteen. He lived in Southern California for a while, and then with friends in Northern California. "I really don't know much about that period in his life," says Gina.

Years later, when Gina was on her way to college, Josh returned home. "He went back to school to get his GED," recalls Bob Prince. "He tried to work. But he couldn't hang on to jobs." He began to hear voices telling him to do strange things, like get rid of all his clothes. "That's when we realized that there was something more going on," says his father. "His thinking just wasn't rational." He checked himself into a mental facility and then, just as quickly, checked himself back out. During one of his manic states, Josh was detained for trespassing and resisting arrest. On several occasions, he threatened his own parents, seemingly oblivious to police officers standing nearby. "He doesn't remember most of that. It was very scary. It could have been a tragic situation." Eventually Josh was incarcerated in a Monterey County Jail, says Robert Prince.

It took me a moment to realize that Bob Prince was crying. "It was kind of a blessing in disguise," he continued, a moment later. "They have a really wonderful program here where they finally understood what's really going on. They've been able to keep him stable and on medication." Gina's brother was even able to travel to Los Angeles and visit his nephew, four-year-old Cassius, who she says, "loves his uncle very much."

* * *

In 1995, Gina began her quest to find her biological parents. It was something she had wanted to do since she was ten but her parents had not supported the search at that time, thinking it would be best to wait until she was older. Now, as an adult, Gina hired a private detective who located her birth mother in Atlanta, Georgia, within forty-eight hours.

She learned that her biological mother had put her up for adoption for many reasons. "She was young, in a bad place in her life, not with my birth father," says Gina, "and her parents were against her having a mixed-race child." She considered having an abortion, but a religious friend convinced her not to. Their relationship started out promising, says Gina, but turned sour when Gina's mother decided not to attend her wedding in 1998. "She just felt like she would be too self-conscious," recalls Gina. "And that kind of pissed me off because I felt like, 'Okay I tracked you down. I flew out to meet you.' It felt like I was doing everything. Even though she seemed happy to meet me, I was putting forth all the effort. So that was kind of annoying. And then she didn't come to my wedding and I just kind of shut it down."

"I suspected it wasn't going as rosy as she had hoped," recalls Maria Prince, adding that her daughter was very disappointed about her birth mother's decision not to attend the ceremony. "I sent her a note once to say 'thank you' for having Gina, and also to invite her to sit with us at the wedding," adds Maria. "But she thought it wasn't the right time."

Gina and her birth mother have not spoken since.

Nor has she been able to find her biological father, mostly because her birth mother claims that she isn't sure of his name. "So that kind of sucks," says Gina. "I guess I really am at a dead end with that because I'd need to contact her again, to ask about the name. My sister Crista was working on it for a while," she adds. "Talking to my birth mother by e-mail. But she got a message from her saying, 'It's just too difficult, so please, just stop asking.'"

When asked if she is close to her sisters, Gina falters. "Uh . . . we don't talk on the phone that often or visit because it's so far," she offers. (One sister lives in Seattle and the other in North Carolina.)

"Years later things come out," says Maria Prince. She recalls a conversation with Gina about the interracial adoption controversy that was then brewing: Congress had attempted to ban "race-matching" by adoption agencies in 1994. Then, in 1995, the popular film *Losing Isaiah* was released. The movie starred Halle Berry as a crack addict whose son was adopted by a white mother, played by Jessica Lange. Gina had called her mother to research the *Sweet Justice* episode she was writing, that delved into the same issue.

In the episode, the white father of two adopted African American children says this: "Charles isn't my black son, he's just my son. His race doesn't matter." Later, another character offers this rebuttal: "Anybody who says they don't see color is lying. We live in a racist society." And in the script, no matter how much Charles tries to deny that his white upbringing didn't have an adverse psychological impact on him, the truth eventually comes out. He doesn't say much when he's in the company of other black people, it seems, because he's afraid they'll find out "how different he is" and that he "doesn't talk the same, act the same, think the same."

Perhaps Gina's own anger about the matter is best summarized in the words of a character named Jordan Downs, a 28-year-old African American attorney. "No one here is questioning that the Perrys are good parents," he argues in the courtroom. "They've provided food, clothing, shelter, love. But is that all that makes a home? Isn't a home also a place where one can grow up with pride . . . where one can come to understand their culture . . .This the Perrys can never provide . . . the moment-to-moment, day-to-day experience of being black in America. [The child] will grow up in a white culture but she is not white. And when she is no longer allowed to ignore she is different from those around her, will she not begin to hate what makes her different?"

"It was back when they were saying black children should be placed in black homes," recalls Maria Prince. Gina had been troubled by depictions of the issue in films like *Losing Isaiah*, which made the white adoptive mother the hero and the black mother the villain. But it was during a conversation with her daughter that Maria Prince explained her own feelings, perhaps for the first time. "I said, 'While this debate goes on children should not be left in foster homes.' I told her she was too important to be left in a foster home. I think that helped her to understand."

Today, Gina realizes that being raised by her parents was better than being placed in foster care. But she also believes that those who adopt children of a different race need to be more aware of the challenges their children will face. In the *Sweet Justice* episode, the Perrys are allowed to adopt a black child in the end, but only if they agree to make fundamental changes in their lifestyle, such as "joining a black church, meeting new friends, and enrolling her in integrated or all-black schools." There are classes that parents need to take in cultural history and sensitivity training, explains Gina. "If it's a Chinese child that they're adopting, then they need to learn about the Chinese culture."

"Absolutely," agrees Maria Prince, adding that such training would have made it easier for her own children. "We were clueless," she admits. "We were kids from the sixties. Idealistic."

* * *

When *Sweet Justice* was cancelled in 1995, after just one season, Gina vowed never to return to television unless she had a "bigger voice." But she did go back, in fact, the very next year, to another multiracial drama called *Courthouse.* "I was excited about that one," she recalls. "It was supposed to be like *ER* in a courthouse, where you follow the judge and the cops."

Moreover, the show had an integrated cast and two black leads—still a rarity in television at the time. "But then the new regime at CBS came in and decided that they couldn't have two black leads in a drama." The pilot was reshot to replace black actors with white ones.

Again, Gina thought of quitting. "I had a long talk with the executive producer. . . . But it was still a pretty multiracial cast, so I ended up staying. And anyway," she adds with a tiny chuckle, "even though they got rid of the black characters as leads, I always made them my focus." Being raised the way she was, offers Felicia Henderson, may have made Gina more dogmatic about how blacks are depicted in film and television. "We disagree for the most part on all that stuff about race. I believe we should be shown in all aspects of our lives—scars and scabs and all. But Gina will say, 'Do you have to show that character in that light?' "

Despite receiving strong ratings, *Courthouse* was also cancelled after just one season. And this time Gina left television for real, determined to focus on the screenplay for her first feature film, *Love & Basketball.*

"I remember one Sunday she invited a group of us to her house to watch the Laker game," recalls close friend Sandra Perez-Thomas (who played a walk-on role in *Love & Basketball* as #18 on the USC team). "As soon as the game ended, she got up and turned off the television. We were all like, 'What's going on?' Kind of dumbfounded, you know. 'Is she gonna put on a movie on or what?' But she was writing *Love & Basketball* at the time, and she was just like, 'I have work to do.' She turned off the TV. Just like that. You guys gotta go."

* * *

"I'm trying to decide how much I want to tell," says Reggie Bythewood, speaking by phone one August evening. "I've gotten more comfortable over the years talking about it." The "it" he is referring to is Hodgkin's disease and his diagnosis came in October of 1997. "Gina was with me when we got the news," he says. "We were engaged then . . . She had already written a couple of versions of *Love & Basketball* so the big thing was getting it to the place where it was good enough to send to Sundance." When Gina got the long-awaited invitation for the coveted film festival, it was at the same time that Reggie was scheduled to begin radiation treatments. "She didn't want me to go through it by myself," recalls Reggie, "and she started to have second thoughts about going to Sundance. But it was never even a question," he adds quickly. "We were just both determined. We really wanted to crack the film circuit."

And they did.

Reggie, who had already written Spike Lee's *Get on the Bus* in

1996, recovered from his illness within the next six months, married Gina, and went on to write and direct *Dancing in September* for HBO in 2000, and *Biker Boyz*, his theatrical directorial debut in 2003. (Gina shares a producer credit on the film.) "Our philosophy was 'tomorrow's not promised,'" he says. "Let's just get married, live our lives, and not wait around for anything." When Gina, then 30, was invited back to Sundance for the highly prestigious Director's Lab in June of 1998, just weeks after their wedding in the lush vineyards of Santa Ynez, California, the couple postponed their honeymoon trip to Ghana, Kenya, and South Africa because without Sundance, *Love & Basketball* might have never been sold.

I first met Gina when I interviewed her in the living room of her suburban San Fernando Valley home. It was April of 2000, just nine hours before the Los Angeles premiere of the film, a semiautobiographical story about a young female athlete who wanted to play professional basketball. Watching the movie later that evening at the Sunset Strip Cinerama Dome I remember being "blown away" (to use one of Gina's favorite phrases) by the way it redefined a woman's inner passion as the source of her outer beauty. Blown away by the way it elevated sweat, grit, and desire (Me'Shell Ndegéocello playing mournfully in the background) over pearls, makeup, and traditional, domesticated femininity.

The film had so many memorable moments that I, as a

cultural reporter, had never before seen onscreen in quite that way. When Monica (Sanaa Lathan) offers Quincy (Omar Epps) her virginity, for example, the range of emotions captured is awesome: fear, tenderness, hope, trust, and surrender, all wrapped into one masterful sequence and reflected back *through a black woman's eyes*. Gina said that she wanted to show the reality of a woman's first time—like having Monica bashfully cover her breasts with both hands during her first moments of nakedness. "For us it hurts," she explained. "It's scary. It shows your vulnerability."

But her script was not an easy sell. It was turned down by every major studio for being "too soft." The industry preferred scenes like the one from the feature film *Soul Food*, they told her, where a black woman chases her husband with a kitchen knife. One executive pushed for the love scene to be more sexual, more "male fantasy." Another even entertained the idea of finding some "hot, young, white" actors to play the lead roles of Monica and Quincy. After two years of writing and nurturing her dream, Gina found herself at a dead end with her screenplay and nowhere else to go.

All that changed when the Sundance Institute invited her to participate in its prestigious Screenwriters and Directors Labs. Because of its support, she received positive feedback and a renewed interest in her revised script. Spike Lee's production company, 40 Acres and a Mule (which had passed on the original version), took another look and liked what it saw. With its backing, Gina was shepherded through to New Line Cinema, where she had what she calls a "dream meeting" with executive Michael DeLuca. She took a deep breath and asked for $10 million to make her movie. Calling it one of the best love stories he ever read, DeLuca gave her $14 million instead. The film won a Sundance Humanitas Prize of $25,000, an Independent Spirit Award for "Best First Screenplay," and made a healthy $27 million in box office receipts to boot.

But that was five years ago. The next time I saw Gina, in the Las Vegas desert, she had yet to direct another theatrical release.

* * *

"We have a phrase," says Reggie. "Gotta go chop some wood." Like last week, he didn't get as much writing done as he wanted to and Gina was in the editing room with *Girlfriends*. So this week his wife returned the favor by suggesting that he "just get away somewhere and chop some wood." He checked into a hotel for a week just to write. "I haven't done that since before we had kids," he said, sounding grateful and relieved.

Much of their marriage is about nurturing and reciprocation. For her husband's last birthday, Gina spent months planning one of the greatest surprises of Reggie's life: a four-day trip with their son Cassius, who is four, to visit with Muhammed Ali, Reggie's lifelong idol and his son's namesake. "I mean what kind of present was that?" says Reggie, still amazed. "She got in touch with Howard Bingham . . . you know, the famous photographer and Ali's best friend? And he plotted with Gina for months to pull this off. Cassius was so excited. He kept saying, "Daddy, it's just you and me on this trip, right?" And I remember Ali was there in the hotel room in Florida, at one point, drawing a picture for Cassius. And Cassius was drawing a picture for Ali. I couldn't believe it. They treated him like their grandson."

The couple is "still trying to figure out the balance," says Reggie, between caring for their sons Cassius (for Cassius Clay) and Toussaint (for Toussaint L'Overture) and their dual careers, but they know it can be done. "We both love our family," says Reggie, "and we both love our work." In fact, they even plan to adopt in the not-too-distant future.

"What's amazing," says film editor Terilyn A. Shropshire (*Love & Basketball* and *Biker Boyz*) is that Gina and Reggie are sounding boards for each other, someone "the other person can trust no matter what." When Gina first came into the cutting room for *Love & Basketball*, Shropshire recalls, "she was filled with nervous anticipation. We were putting in incredibly long hours. Sometimes fourteen at a time and on a couple of occasions where I can remember seeing the sunrise." Finally,

Gina made a copy of the film and took it home for Reggie to watch. His response was, 'What are you worried about? This is going to be great.' She came in the next day like a new person. Like a weight had been lifted off her shoulders."

* * *

"It's killing me not being on set," says Gina, who is sitting on the couch of her Woodland Hills home, tucked far away from the street and hidden behind white rose bushes. "I soooo love the process, and to not have been on set for four years now, that's been very tough."

After the success of *Love & Basketball*, she directed *Disappearing Acts* for HBO, an adaptation of the Terry McMillan novel, starring Sanaa Lathan and Wesley Snipes. Then she signed on to direct a project called *The Killing Season*, based on the book by Los Angeles Times journalist Miles Corwin, about the first year in the life of a rookie female police officer in South Central Los Angeles.

"That was one of the most interesting characters I've ever read," recalls Felicia Henderson. "She was physically strong and very intelligent, but also flawed and trying to find love." In the book, this black female protagonist, Marcella Winn, keeps a sign on her desk that says, "I have PMS and a 9-millimeter handgun with 16 rounds. Any questions?" "It was a character I'd never seen before," says Felicia Henderson, "and wanted very much to see. But *The Killing Season* didn't work out. Felicia's series, *Soul Food*, the longest running hour-long television drama featuring an African American cast, follows the lives and loves of three sisters. "If there is a common thread in all of our work," she adds, speaking of herself, Mara, and Gina, "it's that all three of us are really interested in the depiction of black women. It's something that we all keep going back to."

Next, Gina signed on to rewrite and direct *Bleeder*, a story about a white male police officer who is killed after having an affair with a black officer's wife. "The thing that struck me most about that," she says, "was the relationship between the two wives, a black woman and a white woman. It was such a great relationship. And the cool thing was that they had all started out as white characters. I made one of the cops black to add the full racial tension to it and make it more interesting. But of course, that makes it a harder sell," she adds. "It came really close at two different studios but it didn't go."

Most recently she is working on casting *I Know This Much Is True*, an adaptation of the best-selling novel by Wally Lamb. The story is about identical twins, one of whom is schizophrenic. "I read the script and the book and I loved it," says Gina, who is currently trying to cast the lead actor. Will Smith considered the project. So did Leonardo DiCaprio. One of the things she finds most moving about the story, she says, is that the "so-called healthy twin realizes that his heart and soul are just as sick as his brother's brain."

The life of a director is about waiting, says Terilyn Shropshire. "There are a lot of "nos" and "maybes" and you have to be strong enough to weather that." "Sometimes it's hard," says Gina. "You look around and it seems like everybody's making movies but you. But then you realize, 'If I'd wanted to make crap, I could have.'" She actually stopped going to movies for a while after seeing *Con Air* because "no one was doing anything original." But in 1998, Roberto Benigni's *Life is Beautiful* and Walter Salles' *Central Station* "rebooted" her love of film."

What irks her most, says Felicia Henderson, is losing at anything. "And she will get angry about it. Whether we're playing Liverpool Rummy, or if she can't get the actor she wants. Everything is competitive." That's the fight in her, as the character of Monica's mother says in *Love & Basketball.* Gina, like Monica, had also hoped to play professional basketball, but she let the dream slip away after she failed to be recruited by UCLA. It had always been a regret of hers, she said. "Not trying because of the fear." Making *Love & Basketball* helped her to let go of that regret, and to see that there must be both the fight and the surrender in every woman's life. I, for one, will always remember how she created for us a vision of strength in black womanhood that had never been seen before. She created Monica, she says, "so that "black teenage girls could have someone, or something to look up to."

"That was my goal," she adds.

"I hope filmmaking can be that good again."

2

Rest In Peace

SAKIA GUNN

LOVER

Newark, New Jersey

U p a winding staircase in a modest, working-class home in Newark, New Jersey, there is a sloping attic bedroom that was once shared by a fifteen-year-old West Side High School student, Sakia Gunn, and her then nine-year-old sister, Nikyah. A white tank top is tacked up over what used to be Sakia's twin bed, across from a picture of her baby brother, and posters of R. Kelly, Brandy, and Aaliyah. The shirt features an image of Sakia wearing four small studs in her left ear, a nose ring, and a gold hoop in one eyebrow, beside the letters "R.I.P." A small black mole that she hated is barely visible on her nose. And then there's that smile: a perfect feature in this young girl's face.

Sakia's aunt, Bonnie Gunn, a nursing school student and computer technician, lives here with Sakia's grandmother and has more photos in an album. There is Sakia as a younger girl, dressed in a private school blouse and skirt. And another with her friend, Spanky Ross, who "looks white," says Bonnie, "but you'd never know it if you heard her speak. Mommy, is Spank white?" she calls down to Thelma Gunn, Sakia's grandmother and legal guardian, who favors Rosa Parks. (Sakia's mother is a less frequent presence in the home.) "Puerto Rican," is the answer sent back through the hallways. Spanky had been with Sakia and the other girls on that fateful night in the city, but had left early, headed toward Brooklyn.

* * *

"Yo, shorty, come here," called a twenty-nine-year-old man named Richard McCullough. He wore his hair in thick cornrows and was missing two front teeth. "We wanna talk to you," he said getting out of a white station wagon. He worked at White Castle or spinning records but mostly he was known as "the weed man." His associate, Allen Pierce, wore a baseball cap.

"We're gay," said the girls. "We're not interested."

"Oh, you think that's cute?" snapped the man.

The comment wasn't meant to be cute. It was a fact.

The girls referred to themselves as "AGs" or "aggressives," the current term for what used to be known as "butch" lesbians. Sakia, who was not one to waste time in the closet, announced her sexual orientation to her mother Latona Gunn, at age eleven. She "liked girls," she said simply. Over the next few years, she enjoyed passing for a boy among strangers. The young ladies were attracted to "T" as she called herself, referring to her male alter ego, Tyquinne Aleante Gunn. Even grown women would call the house, unaware that the smooth-talking "T" was actually an adolescent girl. "They were always surprised," says her aunt Bonnie. But Sakia got a real kick out of the question, "Are you a boy or a girl?"

"She sure did," agrees Thelma Gunn. "She liked it."

Her mother, Latona, told Sakia to wait until she got older. Her aunt Bonnie tried to get her to dress her like a girl, but that didn't work. Thelma Gunn agreed to buy her granddaughter's school clothes from the men's section of the department store, as Sakia requested. Only occasionally would she ask that Sakia "tone it down"with her masculine look. She played on three different basketball teams and dreamed of being recruited by the WNBA. "She was always in the park with the guys," recalled her cousin, Anthony Hall, "always with a basketball under her arm." In one rare photo, the outlines of Sakia's body can be seen clearly, her sweatpants and workout bra in motion against a flat, muscular stomach and athletic frame.

Valencia Bailey was Sakia's closest friend. Valencia's mother Gail Guions, forty-nine, still remembers how Valencia came home from school the day they met in sixth grade: "Ma! Ma!" she said, so excited. "I met a new friend today. She's just like me." She was "short, light-skinned, and always wore a doo rag," recalls Valencia. The girls called each other affectionate names like "punk" and came out to each other at the age of eleven. "It's like when you know somebody's gonna call you," says Valencia. "And then they call." The girls who looked alike and dressed alike didn't even need words to convey the message. "It was like, 'You, too?'" recalls Valencia. "And 'Yeah, me too.'" Their bond wasn't sexual. As two aggressives, they dubbed themselves "God-cousins." They were players together, says Valencia. Then, to make sure I grasped the full meaning of her words she added, "Roof, roof," to indicate that they could be every bit the "dogs" that men were, having sex with several women at the same time.

At sixteen, Sakia was reportedly engaged to a girl named Jamon Marsh, but was dating Toni Nickerson, too. Jamon knew about the others and told Sakia "as long as you come home to me." The plan was that Valencia and Sakia would marry their respective girlfriends, raise their children together, and of course, play in the WNBA. That was the dream. They were inseparable, celebrating their shared birthday month in May, playing basketball day and night, smoking cigarettes, and hanging out at the African Globe, a downtown Newark night-club frequented by gay teens.

"Sakia *lived* here," says Valencia's mother Gail, a postal letter carrier who is also a lesbian. We were sitting in the living room of the home she shared with her daughter, on the far west side of Newark. "Kia would be in the house before Valencia even got home, standing in the kitchen saying, 'Auntie. Whatchu cooking today?'" Perhaps it was because her own family had a hard time accepting her homosexuality that Sakia felt more at ease here. "Cool ain't the word," says Valencia, when I ask about her relationship with her mother. "She's like my sister."

"I think I did a real good job," says Gail. "None of my kids are crazy." Valencia's father, Darrell, also a letter carrier, remains a close friend of Gail's, just as they were long before their daughter was born. The couple had worked together at a factory in Bloomfield, New Jersey, and took the test to become postal workers at the same time. Gail, who is the mother of two sons as well (one transsexual and the other straight) says that Darrell (not the father of Gail's boys) is an excellent parent to Valencia. Their close-knit family works, she says "because everybody accepts everybody the way they are."

"Some kids aren't as lucky," offers Laquetta Nelson, a local gay activist and family friend. "Their parents think they can beat it out of them. In fact, there's a large homeless community in Newark of gay youth who've been put out," she adds. "I'm very concerned about them."

Valencia's home, in contrast, was a haven, where the girls would eat, sleep, and watch movies together. By her estimation, she and Sakia watched their all-time favorite *Love & Basketball* over a hundred times. "Three times a day sometimes," she says. The movie opens with a tree-lined residential street in Los Angeles and a large, yellow Mayflower truck. As eight-year-old Monica's family moves into their new home, Monica, who wears her unkempt, flyaway hair hidden under a baseball cap, approaches a group of boys shooting hoop. "Girl can't play no ball!" shouts one of the boys. "Ball better than you," responds Monica calmly, as she then proceeds to out-hoop the boys.

"I loved that movie!" says Valencia, "Because it showed that girls can play even when boys don't believe it. I had to go through that, too," she adds. "It was so relevant to me." When she tells me this, I'm reminded of another scene in the movie. The one where Monica is an angry teenager, chiding her mother for thinking she's a lesbian simply because she likes sports. "That's not funny," responds her mother, who is setting the table for dinner. "Well, that's what you think, isn't it?" retorts Monica. "Just because I'd rather wear a jersey than an apron?"

Love and basketball weren't the only things that united Sakia and Valencia.

"They finished each other's sentences," says Gail, waving a slim hand with manicured white fingernails in my direction, to indicate a new thought. "You know how twins do? That's how they were." In fact, Sakia was born at 11:59 P.M. on May 26, 1987. Not far away, at 7:25 A.M. the next morning, Valencia came into the world to join her. They even bickered and fought like sisters. Usually it wasn't about anything serious (except the time they stopped speaking briefly in eighth grade over a girl). It was more like, "Go get me some cereal. No, you go," recalls Valencia. Or, "Run the bathwater. No, you run it." Or, "That's my shirt. Well, then gimme back my jeans." They may have even had such a conversation on the very night of Sakia's death. When they hit the streets, Sakia was wearing Valencia's new sweat suit while Valencia had on Sakia's hooded sweatshirt, jeans, and cleated boots.

While hers certainly wasn't the only murder of a young black teen to take place during those early morning hours on Mother's Day of 2003, it was a uniquely troubling one. A hate crime against a fifteen-year-old girl, Sakia Gunn was the youngest African American ever to be killed for being a lesbian. Her story doesn't fit the usual homicide statistics of drive-bys and drug-related murders. The overwhelming majority of homicide victims are adults killed with handguns. Sakia's death was disquieting, and so oddly unexpected.

It was a Saturday night. Sakia and four friends had spent the evening partying at Chelsea Piers in Manhattan. Just after 3:30 A.M., they took the PATH train back to Newark and walked the four long city blocks to the bus stop. They were five girls in all, standing at the corner of Broad and Market. During daylight hours the intersection was crowded with bootlegged CDs on sidewalk tables and strawberry incense-scented air. Young men filled these corners wearing hooded sweatshirts and baggy pants and passing plastic baggies from palm-to-palm. Oddly, in an age of mobile communication, there were still six pay phones lining the corner, all of them broken. A police booth sat directly across from the bus stop, but it was usually empty by sundown. The girls were waiting there, across from the empty police booth near the broken pay phones, when two men in a white station wagon approached.

"You the ringleader?" asked the man, directing his questions to the boyish-looking Sakia. "I got scared right away when they pulled up," recalls Valencia. "My stomach started hurting."

"I should knock yo ass down right now," continued the man still focused on Sakia. That's when Kahmya Buchanan, seventeen, started "running off at the mouth," recalls Valencia. The man put her in a chokehold "until she was foaming at the mouth." Later, after she was released, the man called out to Sakia.

"Yo, come here," he said.

She did not move.

"Yo, come here," he repeated. According to Valencia, Allen Pierce had lost interest in the situation and returned to his car. But Richard McCullough wouldn't let it go.

"No, I don't gotta come," said Sakia. "You ain't my father."

"That's when he just ran up on her and put the knife to the back of her neck," recalls Valencia, "and they just started spinning in circles." McCullough stabbed Sakia in the chest.

A dreadlocked brown-skinned youth known as Musaf was the first to drive by on the quiet streets not long after the stabbing. "Help!" cried Valencia, banging on the door of his van. On the way to the hospital, she whispered in Sakia's ear, "Keep breathing. Just keep breathing." Later, when she was told that her best friend was dead, Valencia fainted on the hospital floor. Sakia's grandmother went into cardiac arrest.

According to FBI statistics, assaults triggered by sexual orientation are on the rise, at nearly 17 percent of all hate crimes in 2002. That same year, the number of sexual-orientation crimes against victims under the age of eighteen also increased, by 169 percent, while the number of victims under the age of thirty increased by 17 percent. According to the National Coalition Against Violence, perpetrators of hate crimes do not even necessarily differentiate between sexual identity and gender identity, which means that a girl who merely dresses like a boy is also at risk for assault. As the average age for coming out continues to drop each year (it is currently sixteen) and the number of high school students who identify themselves as gay or lesbian rises (it is currently 6 percent), teens like Sakia and Valencia are making their way through adolescence more determined than ever to be who they are. At the same time, they are putting themselves at greater risk for doing so.

"One trend we're seeing," says Clarence Patton, Executive Director of the National Coalition of Antiviolence Programs in New York (NCAVP), "is that there are fewer people committing these hate crimes but they seem to be more brutal." Patton calls these perpetrators "the true believers." In other words, they are "diehard homophobes who are deeply angered by the fact that lesbians and gays are gaining ground in the mainstream public opinion."

West Side High School overlooks the Fairmont Cemetery, a seemingly endless expanse of tombstones that stretches for miles in one of the most high-crime cities in America. Just weeks after her murder, students at West Side leaned out the windows from their classrooms, shouting down toward her gravesite, "Happy Birthday, Sakia!" For them, death was already a routine part of life. Two years earlier, another student had been murdered for his jacket. More recently, a young West Side girl had died after a man passing in the street used her body as a human shield against gunshots. Being a lesbian, being African American, and living in Newark; being bold and aggressive, all added up to one fate for Sakia Gunn: her life rested squarely at the intersections of empowerment and vulnerability.

Perhaps this is why her death carries such a disquieting message. Maybe, if we look closely, the tragedy has something new to tell us about the unexpected twists and turns of hatred in this country.

While there are no available national figures that break down hate crimes by both race and sexual orientation, research compiled by the NCAVP shows that one quarter of lesbian-gay-bisexual-transgender (LGBT) hate crimes have involved lesbians as victims. As Patton points out, however, this figure may not tell the full story. Lesbians are relatively invisible and young lesbians of color even more so. How many black lesbians have been killed for being black, how many for being gay, and how many for being women? We just don't know.

Sakia Gunn's life was "at the intersection of multiple structures of domination," says Patricia Hill Collins, author of *Black Sexual Politics.* "She was black, female, young, lesbian." And there's a class issue, too, says Collins. "If those girls had money they would have driven that night, and this entire incident wouldn't have happened. The class issue means that they were more available to be approached."

Three days after the murder, Newark police obtained an arrest warrant for twenty-nine-year-old Richard McCullough on charges of unlawful possession of weapons, bias intimidation, aggravated assault, and first-degree murder. Prosecuting district attorney, Thomas McTigue, maintained that McCullough had shouted antigay epithets that night. "Look," he said with a world-weary shrug when I spoke to him at the courthouse. "The men were drinking beer and tried to pick the girls up. That's it."

Richard McCullough's family disagreed, of course. In fact, according to his mother, Benita McCullough, Richard's grandmother, Joyce Phillips, was a lesbian who lived in Jersey City with her lover, Joyce Stevens, until her death in August of 2001. Richard often visited the couple as a boy, she explained. "So how could he be biased?" (I was unable to locate Joyce Stevens to confirm this anecdote.) Nekeida Galigher, the mother of McCullough's three-year-old son, called Sakia's death "a freak accident." Galigher, a twenty-six-year-old hospital food service worker, said that she lived with McCullough for six years, from the time she was sixteen to the age of twenty-two. "He's not a gay-basher," she said. "I've even taken him places with people in the life and he never said nothing. We had a ball. They're painting a picture that he's a bad guy," she added, shaking her head. "He's not a bad guy."

Nor was Sakia a bad girl.

She was popular and outgoing and her funeral drew a crowd of twenty-five hundred mourners and friends—a wide range of fellow athletes from all the local high schools, as well as acquaintances from New York City. But like many of her aggressive friends, she didn't look like our stereotypical notion of an innocent victim, notes Kim Pearson, assistant professor of English at the College of New Jersey. "She was not traditionally feminine. She was out late at night. She was gay and she fought back when attacked." This reminded me of another photo in her aunt's album. It is an image of Sakia wearing her usual, "wife-beater" tank top and doo rag, and defiantly offering up the "F-finger" with both hands. Sakia had two sides, says Valencia. "She was loving, caring, devoted. And she was also very stubborn."

"That's why I think so many young folks of color have seized on this," offered Clarence Patton. "Sakia illustrates the dangers of being out without apology." Hopefully, say some, her murder will serve as a wake-up call for Newark's African American community. A candlelit vigil in June of 2003 was followed by a protest rally at City Hall, where participants gathered to raise awareness about the need for stronger legislation to protect gays and lesbians. "The good side of this, if there is a good side," offered Cory Booker, former city councilman and Newark mayoral candidate, "is that there was a real mobilization of the gay community in this city."

"Sharpe James was shocked!" recalls Valencia's mother, referring to the longstanding current African American mayor of

Newark, who had promised to build a center for gay youth in the months after Sakia's murder, but never did. "The gay community didn't even know there were that many people in the gay community!" she adds excitedly. After Sakia's death, Valencia and Gail were suddenly thrust into the broadcast news spotlight. "It was media, media, media," says Gail. "Cars and hotels, and all these different gay organizations sending us to Philadelphia, New York, Massachusetts and Washington, D.C."

For Laquetta Nelson, a forty-eight-year-old bus driver and founder of the New Jersey Stonewall Democrats, Sakia became a symbol. "I grew up in Washington, D.C.," she said, "when terms like 'bull dagger' and 'dyke' were something filthy. Lesbians my age could not have been so brave and outspoken at the age of fifteen because we knew that we would have been found dead someplace. Coming out is an ongoing process," she adds. It was a process that began for her when she was married but away, in the army. "It's about coming to terms with who you are and what your life should be. For Sakia to have arrived at such a knowing so early in life, and to have the courage to speak her truth, touched me deeply," explained Laquetta. In the weeks after her murder, the activist launched the Newark Pride Alliance, which she hoped would become a safe haven for LGBT youth to find refuge from the harsh city streets.

Gail agrees that Sakia represents a new day. As she told *Gay*

City News, "I couldn't go to my mother thirty-five years ago and tell her I was gay. She would have had me in a straight-jacket in an insane asylum. But when Diana Ross sang that song "I'm Coming Out," she added, "people started falling out of the closet!"

Counting on her fingers, Valencia guesses she has had at least nine schoolteachers in grades K–12, who were gay or lesbian. One of these was, of course, Sakia's favorite teacher, thirty-one-year-old Shani Baraka, a coach at West Side High and the daughter of New Jersey former state poet laureate, Amiri Baraka. Shani Baraka was also murdered, in August of 2003, along with her thirty-year-old lesbian partner, Rayshon Holmes, at the home of Baraka's half-sister, Wanda Wilson Pasha during a domestic violence-related incident. In July of 2005, a jury in Middlesex County, New Jersey, found James Coleman, also known as El-Amin Pasha, guilty of two counts of murder. It is believed that he went to the home to kill his estranged wife, but finding her absent, killed Baraka and Holmes instead.

Gail remembers a few teachers of her own back in the day. "There was one who would have the pointer in one hand," she says, standing to demonstrate with a limp-wrist, exaggerated pose, and laughing. "He wore these salmon-colored shirts . . . when it wasn't even the season for salmon shirts!" Gay and lesbian schoolteachers and neighbors and family members have always been in the community, say Gail and Valencia.

At her funeral, an altar to Sakia Latona Gunn was covered with flowers and epithets like "rainbow thug" and "2 gay 2b forgotten" from all those who hoped that her death would carry a deeper meaning for their own lives. Someone offered up two empty Hennessy bottles and a quote from Matthew 5:44. "Do good to anyone who hates you," read the message. "And pray for those who carry you away by force and persecute you."

Two years after Sakia's murder, Richard McCullough, who eventually pled guilty to aggravated manslaughter, assault, and bias intimidation, quietly accepted his twenty-year sentence without fanfare or protest. (Allen Pierce accepted a plea bargain in exchange for testifying against McCullough.) Jamon Marsh, Sakia's fiancé, and Toni Nickerson, one of her many lovers, both graduated from high school, and Jamon enrolled at a local community college. And in June of 2005, a New Jersey state court of appeal ruled, once again, against recognizing gay marriage. Life went on without Sakia. But nothing was the same for Valencia Bailey.

In the summer of 2005, when I visited Valencia and Gail in their Newark home, Valencia was a high school graduate on her way to Morgan State University in Maryland, planning to major in computer science and pursue her dream of playing in the

WNBA. She was also in love and engaged to be married to Atiya Wells, seventeen, who wore a diamond ring and a black miniskirt. Valencia, still AG, wore baggy pants, thick, auburn-colored dreadlocks, and a backward baseball cap. Her arms were covered with tattoos. There were the letters "R.I.P." above Sakia's name, written in rainbow-colored script; the dates "5/26/87–5/11/03"; a basketball and the inscription "WNBA #3"; the letter "A" for her brother (a transvestite named Danielle); an "L" for her straight brother Lawrence; and her own initials, "VJB." On her back appeared the name "April," ("An ex-girlfriend, but I'm gonna fix that," she said, with a quick glance toward Atiya); and across her waist, a chain-link design encircling her like a belt, with an intricate padlock at the center; a woman's face with long hair and the name, "Atiya."

When Sakia was killed, said Valencia, taking herself back to that time, "I wanted to drop out of school, kill myself, give up. Fuck life. What's the point?" In fact, she had told me at that time that she didn't think she would ever celebrate her birthday again. And when Valencia graduated from high school, she attended the ceremony only reluctantly, at her mother's urging, and clinging to a laminated picture of Sakia which she held against her chest as the class paused in a moment of silent reflection.

"I thought I was gonna have to put her on medication," said Gail.

"Only one person brought me back," recalled Valencia, glancing at Atiya. "I loved her from that first day I saw her. I was just flabbergasted. I had never been so goo-goo, gaga before. I went up to her and said, 'I like your socks.'"

"What a come-on line," offered Gail in mock disgust.

"She was so beautiful," continued Valencia. It was Atiya who forced her to fill out her college applications and helped her to believe in the future again. "I still get depressed sometimes," added Valencia. "And then I just look in her eyes and it brings me back."

"Go, Smooth!" said Gail, offering a kiss of her own hand and throwing it in Atiya's direction.

People need to get over their homophobia, noted Valencia, when I mention that New Jersey will not recognize her plans for a gay marriage. "They need to just let us live. Besides, if we can't marry here, we'll just go to Vermont." When I asked if she's worried about being out as a young college student at a traditionally black college, Valencia was just as fearless as I imagine Sakia would have been in the same situation. "No," she said plainly. "I'll be fine."

What Valencia did worry about though, was being so far away from her girl, who would be in Washington, D.C., attending Howard University and preparing for a career in nursing. Atiya, who is traditionally feminine, with a delicate, soft-spoken manner and long, thin braids, wore a more moderate collection of tattoos: the name "Valencia" across her abdomen and a Pisces sign on her right thigh. Both women, who often reached across the couch to touch fingertips and palms together as they talked, admitted that they were most afraid, not of what the world thought of them, but of what time and distance might do to their bond.

"She in love," offered Gail, fake-suppressing a smile. "Goofy." And so was Gail for that matter, with her own plans to marry her lover in the near future (a mortician who was sleeping in the next room). As I prepared to leave them, late on this humid summer evening, the forty-nine-year-old mother of three and lover of one suddenly looked as young and vulnerable as her daughter. "So whatchu think of our little family?" she asked cheerfully, her eyes gently searching my own. I could only think of one word, and so I said it.

"Sweet."

3.

Mia Lynn Clark holds a photo of her older sister who died
of complications from AIDS.

Activist

Quincy, Florida

A t the corner of West Crawford and South Jackson streets, in a dusty Florida town called Quincy, sits a dirt lot large enough to hold twenty cars, surrounded by an eight-foot-high fence. Next door is a drive-through liquor store whose owner, an East Indian man named Yogi, shelled out $1,500 for the fence and a pair of Porta Pottis so that his full-time customers could have a place to hang. On any given day or night, Quincy Liquors's most hardcore patrons—crack addicts, moms, laborers in uniform, alcoholics, retirees, teenage truants, and streetwalkers—can be found within the fenced enclosure. On one humid weekday afternoon in August, there are faded pickup trucks and Cadillacs parked inside with their doors open, seats reclined, and music blasting. Some two dozen men and women drift to the store and back. They smoke cigarettes or marijuana, hunkering down on plastic milk crates and talking. Others sit quietly under a large shady tree staring blankly into space as half-pints of liquor in paper bags are passed from mouth to mouth.

Quincy is not the place that usually comes to mind when one thinks of Florida. Far from the Caribbean vibrancy of Miami or the Disney cheerfulness of Orlando, this sleepy town lies hard against the Georgia border in the northernmost region of the panhandle. Like many small southern towns, Quincy doesn't have much to show for itself: scraps of tomato and mushroom farms worked by mostly migrant workers, a few clay mines, and the 384-inmate Quincy Correctional Institution on the outskirts of town.

"Hey, you nice-dressing muthafucka!" slurs a woman standing at the edge of the enclosure to a man wearing a crisp yellow shirt and matching shorts. He smiles as he crosses the cement lot, but keeps on. "I done stopped drinking!" she calls after him, hiding a bottle behind her back. "I ain't tryin' to start no shit," she adds with a lopsided grin.

Folks here know one another by face if not full name. In a place like Quincy it's hard to keep secrets. But this town keeps one little-known fact under wraps: Of 7,500 residents (64 percent African American, 32 percent white, 7 percent Latino, and 3 to 4 percent Asian or Pacific Islander), 130 were infected with HIV in 2002. Of these 117, or 90 percent, were African American, the majority of them women. Unfortunately, when it comes to who gets AIDS Quincy is typical.

The rate at which American women are developing AIDS has more than tripled since 1985, with African American women representing 64 percent of newly diagnosed HIV infections among United States women. Together, African American and Latina women make up 83 percent of all AIDS cases among women in this country, even though both groups together represent a combined total of only 25 percent of American women. "I have not heard those numbers with respect to African American women," said Dick Cheney infamously, during a vice presidential debate in 2004, "I was not aware that it was—that they're in epidemic there, because we have made progress in terms of the overall rate of AIDS infection."

The problem, of course, is not only impacting black women. Overall, African Americans are at least ten times more likely to die from HIV/AIDS than whites and the reported rate of AIDS cases among all African Americans is eight times that of whites. Black youth are an especially disturbing category, comprising 65 percent of all HIV/AIDS cases under the age of nineteen. But exactly why the small-town south has become such a hotbed for AIDS and other sexually transmitted diseases, particularly among heterosexual black women, remains unexplained. While cities like New York, Los Angeles, and San Francisco are at the top of the list for overall reported AIDS cases, among men and women of all races, there is something unique happening among southern women in particular. According to 2003 figures from the Centers for Disease Control and Prevention (CDC) and Kaiser Family Foundation, eight of the ten states with the highest AIDS case rates among women (of all races) are currently in the South: District of Columbia, Maryland, Delaware, Louisiana, Georgia, South Carolina, Mississippi, and Florida. Many of these states of course, have large numbers of African Americans.

Most experts cite poverty, poor educational standards, and lack of access to basic health care as reasons for the spread of the epidemic here. In Gadsden County, Florida, household incomes average below $25,000 and one third of all children live in poverty. A February 2005 study published by the CDC looking at HIV infection among black women in North Carolina, found that recently HIV-infected women were less likely to have discussed sexual issues with male partners and that their reasons for not doing so included financial dependence, low self-esteem, feelings of invincibility, and alcohol and drug use. The study also found that "despite high levels of risk behavior among study participants, more than half of women perceived themselves to be at low risk for infection." Other studies have found similar perceptions to be common across the country.

Similarly, the average black woman in Quincy still refuses, for many reasons, to believe that AIDS can happen to her, even after a wave of media attention to the so-called "down-low syndrome" whereby men have sex with other men but keep the fact a secret from their female partners. Black women readers nationwide were fascinated by novelist E. Lynn Harris's fictional descriptions of such men in books like *Invisible Life* and *Just As I Am,* and yet many continued to ignore the possibility that the men they were themselves dating may have been lying to them. "We as black women often don't know who we're sleeping with," says Temple O. Robinson, M.D., an internist formerly in private practice in Quincy. "Most black men will admit to being a thief, a drug addict, and a wife beater before they'll admit to being bisexual."

If part of the problem is men who lie about their sexual activity, women are guilty of refusing to question their partners. Some are simply afraid to know the truth or afraid of rumors, says Dr. Robinson. Other women are in monogamous relationships and have *no idea* that they're positive. "They may have had three lovers in the past three years," she says. "They come in for a little vaginitis and find out they're HIV-positive. Or you'll have a forty-six-year-old schoolteacher who thinks she has chronic fatigue syndrome and tests positive for HIV." Robinson, who has been in practice for thirteen years says that although she loves caring for patients, she plans to take a rest from the "bureaucracy" of medicine to spend some time with her husband and teenage son.

With so few black doctors in practice in rural communities, and even fewer like Robinson, who are willing to work with large numbers of AIDS patients, there remains the problem of mistrust of medical professionals within black communities. Among the Haitian populations of Belle Glade and Palm Beach for example, says Ronald Henderson, statewide minority AIDS director of the Florida Department of Health, trust has been a big problem. "Before we got the oral swab, we'd come in and they thought we were injecting them with the virus. You couldn't pay them to take the test. And I do understand the mistrust."

Other researchers have looked more broadly at "structural violence" in the lives of women of color, including overlapping causes such as the disproportionate rates of incarceration among black men, poverty, and limited access to health services. In 2002, the overall rate of confirmed AIDS cases in prisons was nearly 3.5 times the rate in the general population, according to Department of Justice statistics. Tellingly, 3 percent of all female state prison inmates were HIV positive, as compared to just 1.9 percent of males. During the March 2005 "Women and AIDS tour," international experts from the United States, Africa, Asia, Latin America, and the Caribbean agreed that economic opportunities were a major piece of the HIV/AIDS puzzle. Structural poverty is definitely a factor, says Ron Henderson. "People forget that with welfare reform, you have a lot of women who've been dependent for a long time. In a town like this, where they can only get a minimum wage job, they were actually living better with food stamps and medical. Now they've started to have 'survival sex' just to pay the rent."

For all these reasons, this story is perhaps most of all about women who, in some deep part of themselves, are afraid of being whole. They have no idea what wholeness would look like inside. And are unsure whether or not they even deserve it.

* * *

At Quincy Liquors, Sondra Jones Anderson, an AIDS education worker, is making her usual rounds. Wearing a silk scarf over her long braids and a black T-shirt that reads, "Investing in Our Youth" (the nonprofit community advocacy group that pays her salary), Sondra has the look and energy of a woman far younger than her fifty-something years. Scanning a stack of manila folders, she pulls one out and calls a man's name. He approaches her in a far corner of the enclosed lot with trembling lips and hands. "Florida law says I'm supposed to just show you this," says Sondra quietly, circling the word "negative" on the document and writing the word "no" beside it. Almost immediately the man's trembling ceases. But Sondra, who wears two pairs of eyeglasses tucked into her shirt collar and one sliding halfway down her nose, is not yet finished with the man.

Sondra's father, a community activist since the early days of the civil rights movement, was a former steward in a laundry turned labor union president. When he married his second wife, the officiator of the ceremony was none other than the Reverend Martin Luther King, Sr. himself. "I grew up in the movement," says Sondra. As a teenager, she recalls registering black voters and marching with her cousins and other relatives for desegregation at a Woolworth's lunch counter in Tallahassee. She remembers when the family had to hide her aunt, an activist, for a time. "I just thought she was staying in this place and that place," says Sondra. It wasn't until later that she realized her aunt was in hiding for registering people to vote. Later, her own husband became active on labor issues as well because, as she puts it, she "wasn't going to be with no man that didn't support the union."

Her mother, who separated from her father when Sondra was twenty-three, was a devout Pentecostal nurse who cared for AIDS patients at a home long before hospices accepted them. Sondra's mother was nevertheless unable to relate to her own children, or talk to them about intimacy in any meaningful way. "My mother was very religious," she recalls, and even more so after the divorce. "She was always throwing oil and reciting verse . . . staying in church half the day and half the damn night . . . and I'd ask, 'Why you in church that long for? You didn't murder anybody.' But she was just trying to serve the Lord." And when she wasn't in church, says Sondra, her mother was mopping and cleaning. "A clean fanatic."

"She never had *any* kind of conversation with me about sex," recalls Sondra. "I remember asking as a teenager, 'How do you have sex and not get pregnant?' Her response was, 'You don't need to know that.' And she was a nurse!" Sondra shakes her head in disbelief. "I've never forgotten that." As well-intentioned as her mother may have been, Sondra believes that young women need to arm themselves with information.

When asked about her own religious beliefs, she says, "I have a personal relationship with God, and I have been baptized, and I confess my sins." Then, turning lighthearted she adds, "I need to do that more often because I sin a lot. It's like a comedian I heard one time who said, 'I have to go to church a lot because I did a lot of sinning. And I know I have some shit planned for the weekend."

In nearby St. Hebron, her large extended family farmed sugarcane "with the mule walking all day long making the syrup." She never knew any of her family members to live in subsidized housing, she says. Everyone owned their own land. Acres of it. There was a time, she says, when it seemed like the whole town was nothing but relatives. In the countryside they organized massive family picnics with hundreds of relatives and games and raffles. Her family would cook "roasted squirrel, raccoon, possum, deer, armadillo, alligator, turtle, chicken, hog, wild turkey, bear." Basically anything "that came through the woods, or run cross the road. Put some ice on it for later." I'm trying to figure out if she's pulling my leg when she adds, "They even ate the liver and light" of a hog . . . I don't even know what the light is, but I think it's illegal. We called that 'hasher' and ate it right there, immediately after they kill the hog. If it was a male, we ate the nuts. They called that 'mountain oysters.'"

When Sondra had children of her own, a daughter when she was twenty and a son at twenty-eight, they were raised "on her hip" while she attended rallies, walked picket lines, and studied at Florida A&M University. In 1980, the year her son was born, Sondra was instrumental in sending "the first all-black delegation to the Democratic Party from Gadsden

County." She says that no other all-black delegation from Florida has gone since. And her children were by her side when she ran for public office as the Gadsden County Supervisor of Elections. "I won the primary but in the second election they did a manual absentee ballot count and 125 votes were thrown out." She was only seventy-three votes short. "But that's how they do black people down here," she adds. It was in Gadsden County, after all, with its 57 percent African American population, that one of every eight ballots was thrown out in the infamous Bush-Gore election of 2000. In any case, says Sondra, the defeat taught her a valuable lesson, "I was better at running campaigns than I was at being the candidate."

But watching Sondra work the crowd at Quincy Liquor proves otherwise. It is here that she administers HIV tests, offers counseling on drug and alcohol abuse, and tirelessly lectures young men and women on the dangers of unprotected sex. "My mother saves lives," says her daughter, Precious Anderson-Moore, an attorney in Atlanta. "She's always been out there. Picketing, raising money, giving away money. She has a way of communicating with people on their own level." And she is acutely aware of the need for grassroots advocacy of health care in black communities. "My granddaddy used to drive to Georgia to see a dentist," she recalls, "because it was a black dentist there, Dr. Hutto. Anybody that had transportation would go to Dr. Hutto even if you had to get up at like 4:00 or 5:00 in the morning to get there."

In fact, Sondra's own alarm clock goes off at 4:00 A.M. and the first thing she does upon waking is take a few Anacin tablets for "aches and pains." Her doctor has warned her about her weight and the need to improve her diet and exercise more often. But she doesn't eat breakfast because there's no time. "I just eat everywhere I go . . . just talkin' and eatin' . . . I say, Hey, what you got cooking? Gimme some of whatchu got."

Sometimes, at the end of a long day her son C.J., who is twenty-one, will "whip up some Hamburger Helper." Country picnics are a rare occasion now, and no one has time for standing over a stove. "I have asthma, I'm overweight, and I get stressed a lot," she says. "I know I need to slow down, but I'm okay. I'm not that tired yet."

For now, she lets the pain pills do their work. Within a half hour or so of taking them, she's out of bed and ready to start another day. Packing her laptop computer, she arrives at the office of Investing in Our Youth (IOY), a nondescript building shared with the office of Social Security and the Department of Corrections, usually before 6:30 A.M. Once there, she checks e-mail messages, mostly from the Department of Health or the Department of Justice, having to do with her work on HIV/AIDS prevention and as a mediator for troubled youth. She responds to messages from concerned

parents, grandparents, school administrators, and county officials. Sometimes Sondra has even spent whole evenings
combing the streets, looking for missing or troubled youth
herself. She doesn't get much free time but she likes going on
the Internet and reading, educating herself. Recently, she read
The Pact, the true story of three African American friends who
became doctors in New Jersey.

At the moment though, at Quincy Liquors, Sondra is
making sure she has the undivided attention of the man whose
HIV test results have come back negative.

"This result is good for all the sex you ever had in your life,
up until six months before the day you were tested," she
explains. "You not gonna be using any needles, are you?"

The man shakes his head.

"And you not gonna be sucking nobody's breast milk?"

No again.

"Well, then," she says, staring him in the eye. "The only way
you can get AIDS now is by having unprotected sex."

But there is virtually no one inside the dirt lot who consis-
tently has safe sex. "Men say they 'raw dog' it," says Sondra.
"They tell me, 'Baby, I done drunk so much liquor, I can't even
get it hard enough to put it on.' Or they say the condom isn't
big enough. So I just take out a liter-size bottle of soda and
slip a condom on it. Then I tell them, 'If you got something
bigger than that, well, I just don't know.'"

Angela Turner, a program coordinator at Investing in Our Youth, says that whether or not a woman uses a condom can depend on her relationship. "I hear girls say that they use condoms with the guys on the side but not with their main man. They don't want to use them with the boyfriends because they think that says either, 'I'm cheating' or 'I think you are.'"

Sondra points to another reason.

"We're wondering what makes these girls consider themselves so . . ." Here she pauses, searching for the right word. After a few seconds, she finds it: "Worthless." "It's like they don't think of themselves as important enough. They don't think of themselves as precious." It's not a way of thinking that Sondra can relate to. "There are no unloved people in my family," she explains. "I come from a hell-raising bunch. I was born to raise hell. I think I had one doll my whole life because my mother did not want me to learn [just to raise babies]." Sondra in turn taught her own daughter, a Harvard-educated attorney, the same lesson. (Although now, Sondra half-jokes, she wishes her daughter would give her a few grandbabies.) There is no mistaking the fact that her daughter has been raised to believe. She is precious.

On another afternoon at Quincy Liquors, Sondra's son C.J., a student at Florida State University, takes off his T-shirt and drapes it over his head against the heat, revealing a panther tattoo on his upper arm. Already, Sondra's team of volunteers, including C.J., has nearly met the Department of Health's annual goal of administering one hundred HIV tests, six months ahead of schedule. "Do you ever have sex for drugs or money?" one worker asks a woman being swabbed. "You mean like after I have sex with my husband and then ask him for beer money?" she answers.

If Sondra is the yang approach to AIDS education, always ready to give a safer-sex talk, then Alma Ward-Venisee, founder and executive director of Investing in Our Youth, is the yin. "My approach is total abstinence which I think is best, especially with our young people," says Alma, who became concerned about HIV prevention while working as a program manager in an alternative high school in the late 1990s. "I started watching the girls and how they liked to wear the big pants and big shirts and boots. They were all sexually promiscuous," she says, "and their STD rates were very high." But most of all "they just needed someone to talk to. Some of them were living with their grandparents, with both a mother and a father in prison."

Alma began inviting a few of the girls to her home for Sunday dinners with her husband and children because "I felt they needed someone who cared." Before long she had started what she calls a "female development" program. In the beginning, both Alma (a practicing Christian) and Sondra (who is not) were committed to teaching abstinence only.

"We worked with high school dropouts," says Sondra, "and taught them how to do construction work." They received funding from the Department of Housing and Urban Development and tried to start a charter school. When that didn't work out they experimented with other avenues of youth empowerment and education. Over the years, their partnership has been powerful and lasting. So when the Florida Department of Health offered funding for a comprehensive prevention program including condom distribution, they decided to take the offer.

"Now I'm the condom lady," says Sondra. "I say take the safe-sex information out of the back room and put it out on the kitchen table." In her traveling bag of goods, she carries dildos, Sheer Glyde dental dams, flavored rubbers, female condoms, and all manner of safer-sex paraphernalia. Perhaps more importantly, she teaches women what she calls "negotiation and refusal skills." "I tell these young girls to use condoms. Because if you trust him with your heart and it gets broken, you'll survive. But if you trust him with your life, you don't have another one."

These are controversial lessons, of course, particularly in these times when the Bush administration is intent on squashing any form of sex education or information, other than abstinence. Sondra still struggles to convince religious leaders and school officials to let her give safe-sex lectures. But there is something about one phrase in particular that rings powerful in my head and stays with me long after my visits with Sondra. *"Negotiation and refusal skills."* It occurs to me that we teach our children so many other basic survival lessons—how to budget, how to talk to white people at work, how to stand up for ourselves, how to plan for the future and fill out college applications. Why can't we teach them that they have the right to *negotiate* when, where, and how they have sex? Why can't we teach them that they have the right to say no?

When asked why the Gadsden County school system refused to introduce IOY's safe-sex message into its classrooms, Superintendent Sterling DuPont told me this: "My preference is that we talk about good health [which is] just so much bigger than AIDS. Nutrition is just as important. Exercise is just as important. My philosophy is not to emphasize just one issue."

"I have spoken to Sterling DuPont," retorts Sondra. "And he seemed interested in having me address the staff and students but said he needed to figure how to approach it." Clearly frustrated, she adds, "What's to figure out?"

Then there's the question of black churches, which remain largely silent on the issue of AIDS, with some notable exceptions. Reverend George McRae's Mount Tabor Missionary Baptist Church in Liberty City, Florida, battles what it calls the "triangle of death" in black communities—AIDS, prison, and drugs—while younger brother Reverend Andrew McRae's Faith Tabernacle Baptist Church in Gainesville, Florida, is known as "the condom church" for its distribution of pro-phylactics. At least a third of George McRae's congregation is HIV-positive. "We give them information, home-cooked breakfast, and as much love as possible," he says. "We don't have time for judgment," adds Andrew McRae.

In contrast, Gadsden County has a whopping three hundred plus churches for a population of only about forty-five thou-sand. And yet, one young woman laughed out loud when I asked if her pastor had ever spoken about AIDS from the pulpit. In talking with community members, I was able to identify only one church where the issue had been raised openly, by a man with AIDS named Randall Zeigler ("Miss Zeigler") and the only reason he was allowed to speak there was because his mother was the minister.

"This is the Bible Belt," explains Ronald Henderson. "Because of homosexuality and drugs and other risk factors involved, many churches still feel that people with AIDS have sinned and are getting what they deserve." The "complacency and denial frustrates me," he adds, "because we put a lot of resources into getting the message out. But people are just thinking about how to pay the rent and keep my lights on."

"I believe these girls need to know how to protect them-selves because these men, these predators, don't care about them," says Sondra. "If they did, they would not be having unprotected sex with them. I tell these young girls, 'You gotta love yourself because he might be gone tomorrow. He might drop dead, or you might have to kill him. But you need to take care of yourself.'" The message seems simple enough. So why aren't more young black women getting it?

* * *

Shirley A. Gennie, forty, is sitting upright in her room at Tallahassee Memorial Hospital, a 770-bed facility near Quincy. Because Gadsden Community Hospital (Quincy's only hospital) has no intensive-care unit and does not offer MRIs and CT scans on a regular basis, many patients are sent to Tallahassee Memorial for medical care.

When Sondra and I arrived the first time to talk with Shirley about how she contracted the HIV virus, we found her curled up in a fetal position, suffering from severe stomach pain and unable to talk. Excess fluid around her heart would keep her in and out of Tallahassee Memorial over the next few months, but when we returned the next day, she seemed to be feeling better. Beside her pillow was a stack of compact discs including local favorites like The Jackson Southernaires, Flossie and the Singing Sisters, and Ronica and the Mighty Blazing Stars. I found it hard to imagine Shirley listening to this good-news music with pleasure, or any reaction at all. When asked about her illness, her responses were monosyllabic. Even though she had signed a consent form and agreed to be interviewed, she either didn't trust me, didn't care, or just didn't have anything to say.

"So the man who infected you had done time in prison?"

"Yeah."

"Did you ever talk to him again, after you found out you were HIV-positive?"

"No."

"Why not? You didn't want to?"

"No."

In July of 2002, Florida state put into effect a new law making HIV-testing of every prisoner mandatory sixty days before their release. The law would come too late for Shirley of course. And even if it had been in effect and her partner had known his status, would she have asked? Would he have told her? Would he have used protection to save her life?

We went to see Shirley because her daughter, who is in her early twenties, Shakeithia Deshawn "Shawn" Jones, has AIDS as well. She was tested after coming down with the worst case of herpes her primary care physician had ever seen.

"How do you feel about the fact that you and your daughter are both infected?" I asked Shirley.

"It never came across my mind."

"Well, does it make you sad?"

"No."

"Why not?"

"I never sat down and really thought about it."

"Are you hopeful?"

"No."

"You don't have any hopes—isn't there something you want to happen?"

"I never really thought about it."

Shawn, who also signed a consent form agreeing to be interviewed and to have her photograph taken, was nowhere to be found during my visit. According to her doctors, she was put on a course of treatment, and her condition improved. She gained weight and was looking better, but that didn't last long. Soon, she was "back in the streets." Four months later, in December of 2002, both Shirley and her daughter Shawn died within weeks of one another.

* * *

In another part of town, Linda Nealy invites Sondra and me into her home, an airless, crowded space full of teenagers and children, where we talk about Linda's older sisters, both of whom died of AIDS: one in 1987, at age thirty-seven, and the other in 1998, at age fifty-one. On the day we visited, two of her five children were home: Yolanda Tatum, then nineteen, who had recently given birth to her first child; and another, referred to as Pokey, who sat curled up in a tattered easy chair by the door. (Another daughter, Felesha "Fifi" Tatum, had been missing for many months, and was last seen with two men in a blue Ford Escort with a bumper sticker on the back that said "El Salvador." Her story had received barely a blip of local news coverage.)

One of Linda's sisters was infected by a man who came to work in the area during the tomato season. "Nobody knew he was sick," she says. "I don't think he knew. Because we started taking him to the doctor and he didn't know what was happening, and by the time we found out he already had holes all over his legs." At this, Linda Nealy makes a gagging sound as if fighting back nausea.

Later, Linda's daughters turn the conversation to a recent bit of gossip about a local fourteen-year-old who took a bleach-and-bubble bath after letting men give her "golden showers" (a street term for urinating on a girl's naked body). The girl had dropped out of school. She thought that sterilizing her-self with bleach would prevent diseases and infections.

Whether or not the girl was using drugs they do not know. "We tell people that drugs cloud your mind and you take chances you wouldn't normally take," says Sondra. "Especially when an addict is "jonesing" as they say, or "fiending . . . you might have to go with six or seven men, trickin', just to get a hit. And you'll do anything to get a hit. There are women out there with a man in every hole. All at once, ten men. And for what? A nickel ball. Cuz she jonesing. And then she gotta go right back for some more!"

"Some of these girls aren't even doing this for money to buy drugs," continues Sondra, who has worked herself into a fury by this point. "These younger girls, fourteen and fifteen, are having sex with men for money to get their hair done, to get their nails done, and to go to McDonald's. Stupid stuff. They hang out on the corners on the first of the month when the men get paid." Others don't get anything. "They just allow themselves to get screwed, and when they come home two or three days later, they're hungry, dirty, and nappy-headed. I cannot for the life of me understand," she adds, clearly heartbroken and distressed, "how they can think so little of themselves." The conversation reminds me of all the ways in which AIDS is really about so many other things: poor education and health care, poverty, despair, hopelessness. It's about young women longing for someone to make them feel wanted, if only for a few minutes.

* * *

On the northern side of town, near the elementary school, Rita M. Moore greets us from her desk at the Quincy Recreation

Center. Sondra's son, C.J., grew up playing basketball here, while Rita's daughters, Christine Renee and Mia, kept the game stats. But something went wrong with Renee. It began with marijuana in her teen years. Then, at twenty-three, when she was an army private, a drug test came back positive for marijuana, and she was given an honorable discharge. Later, she "was an avid cocaine addict," says Rita, "with the pipe and all that." By her midtwenties, Renee was back home telling her mother she was sick and wanted to get clean. "Mommy, I want to get my life straight," she said.

"The first thing I did was put her in the bathtub," recalls Rita. And that was when she saw the marks in a "mazelike pattern," all across her back, symptoms of syphilis and, as Rita would later learn, AIDS. When Renee became pregnant despite the diagnosis, she married her child's father and had the baby. Her son lived four months.

In the last two years of her life, Renee suffered from pneumonia and seizures so severe that she had to learn to walk all over again. She had no more fatty tissue in her face and suffered from severe appetite loss and dementia. She once took a bite of a hamburger from Burger King and stuffed the rest of the burger under her pillow. Rita and Mia cared for her at home for three years, which was unusual. Many AIDS patients are abandoned by families who fear being stigmatized or infected themselves. If they do let them stay, says Sondra, "they have to eat with a plastic fork and can't get too close to the children. They'll hide them away and tell people they have cancer."

But Rita would do no hiding of her Renee. "God is *good* to me," she explained. "And I don't have to hide my head to nobody. That was my *baby*. And I'll go on loving her until the good Lord calls me home."

Toward the end of her life, says Mia, her sister was completely blind. At this memory, her eyes fill with tears. "She would just sit two inches from the television screen with her eyes wide open, rocking back and forth."

Renee died in 1996, at the age of thirty-five. "When they say you 'deteriorate,'" says Rita, "they're not lying." When asked why her daughter used drugs and didn't protect her body, she paused for a moment before answering. "She didn't love herself. We talked, we communicated. I read with her and went to different programs . . . I tried to teach her. Now, I just tell these young girls," she adds, wiping back tears. "No matter what he tells you, true love will wait."

* * *

Some stories don't turn out the way you planned. The feature article I eventually wrote about my visit to Quincy was published in the February 2002 issue of *Essence*. Later that year, it won an award for social issues reporting from the New York chapter of the National Association of Black Journalists. We thought it a great success, not only because it illustrated the devastation that AIDS was having on heterosexual black women who did not consider themselves at risk, but also because it honored the work of women like Sondra Anderson and Alma Ward-Venisee.

But although the town had initially welcomed our presence (everyone we spoke to signed full disclosure forms and posed for photographs) some were later outraged that a national publication focused such a "negative" story on their little town. Soon after the article appeared on newsstands, the *Tallahassee Democrat* reported that Quincy was in an "uproar." Mayor Derrick Elias expressed outrage, telling the *Democrat*, "How dare they do a story like this that says we sit around all the time and have sex with each other." Local officials and community members directed their anger and shame toward Sondra and Alma, who reported that the backlash was making it difficult for them to do their jobs.

There were others, however, who publicly supported the work of Investing in Our Youth. Quincy City Commissioner Keith Dowdell told the *Democrat* that "the *Essence* magazine article was a blessing in disguise. We need to work hand in hand to get the problem solved." An editorial in the *Democrat* agreed. Quincy needs to get over its "public relations quibble," it said, and deal with the social stigma, lack of information, and silence associated with HIV/AIDS. "If it's a 'positive' story they want," the editors concluded, "this is their chance to create one."

Within weeks of the article's appearance, some good news made its way back to *Essence* when we heard that school superintendent Sterling DuPont had agreed to allow Sondra to address his staff and students—not with a complete safe-sex message including condoms, but as a beginning. At first, Sondra seemed tentatively hopeful that things might change after all in Quincy.

Three years after the article's appearance, however, Alma Ward-Venisee told me that her organization had not "gotten around the trust issue" and that people in Quincy were still afraid even to speak the words "HIV" and "AIDS." She called on local officials to help with outreach by sponsoring a massive public testing campaign. If they were so supportive of the article, she asked, "Then what are they going to do?"

My attempts to reach Keith Dowdell to pose that question went unanswered—as did my calls to Sondra Anderson. I was saddened that she chose not to speak with me after the many hours we spent talking, riding, and visiting families in Quincy. During our time together we talked about having children, or not having them, the men in our lives, our relationships with our parents, our spirituality, our faith. And we laughed together. I can only hope she knows that I continue to believe in her and in the work that she does.

Ronald Henderson at the Florida Department of Health—the official who had initially suggested Quincy as the location concern for my story told me that it was hard to gauge whether or not AIDS awareness and prevention had improved in Quincy in the intervening years since the article. In terms of pure numbers, the reported HIV cases in Quincy increased marginally between 2002 and 2004, but this could be due to more people being tested and seeing the positive results for old infections, which would be a good thing. A drop in new cases, on the other hand, might not indicate an actual decrease, but might simply be due to the ongoing shame and fear of getting tested, which would be a bad thing. Nothing was what it seemed, and as Spencer Leib of the Department of Health confirmed, there was just no accurate way to measure changes in HIV/AIDS cases in Quincy since 2002.

One positive result of the article though, according to Henderson, was that the Board of Gadsden County Commissioners applied for and received an annual grant of $150,000 for three years in state prevention funds, which it continues to use for street outreach, testing, and public education. "Had it not been for the article, they probably would not have applied."

An official Department of Health statement noted that before the story appeared, very few people in Quincy talked about HIV/AIDS openly and "only in occasional whispers." Some of the DOH funding offered to Quincy has been sub-contracted out to Investing in Our Youth, which will need all the support it can get in its ongoing efforts to educate its community. Most people have simply relied on misinformation from the rumor mill, said Henderson. "Don't date anybody from Quincy. Everybody there has AIDS."

In 2004, 70 percent of all AIDS cases diagnosed among Florida women remained African American, a rate twenty-one times higher than that among white women in the state. About 84 percent of these cases were the result of heterosexual contact.

4.

Lynn Battle, recipient of a Jefferson Award for public service in 1994,
with her mother, Mamie Weeks.

CITIZEN

Birmingham, Alabama

W hen Whitlynn Tia-Juana Battle was a girl, her uncle, Judge J. Richmond Pearson (who would later become Alabama's first black state senator since Reconstruction) used to pick her up from school in the wealthy, all-white suburb of Mountain Brook, Alabama. Since Lynn's mother, a former domestic worker and mother of ten, was busy studying to become a lawyer herself and her father had died when she was six, Uncle Richmond had the responsibility of helping out. But he was never much of "a kid person," as Lynn recalls. His idea of playtime was to put Lynn and her cousin to work helping him research cases in the law library.

And research came easy to Lynn even at a young age. She was smart. In fact, she graduated from high school two years early, after completing the tenth grade, with an almost perfect SAT score. She jokes that school administrators did it just to get rid of her rabble-rousing. Bored and angry in her surroundings, Lynn had started a "Black Studies" group on campus. But since her cousin (the only other black student in the school) refused to attend meetings, she had to recruit white kids to join her at McDonalds for talk of revolution.

After high school, Lynn stayed close to home, attending the small, historically black Miles College. A year later, she transferred to Howard University in Washington, D.C., and eventually, finished her studies at the University of Colorado where she received a Bachelor of Science degree in mathematics and physics. Lynn's family expected her to go on to law school, or to find some other equally respectable career. (Her father was a physics professor and another uncle became Las Vegas's first African American city councilman.) But when Lynn announced her plans to become a photographer, Uncle Richmond was adamant. She would not become a "bum with a camera," as he put it. She would get a "real job."

So Lynn became an accountant, which she hated, because she "couldn't figure out what the hell else to do." She moved to San Francisco where she worked on a commercial office park and residential development that would eventually become occupied by a mostly Asian American community. In her work, she was often outdoors "in the dirt checking up on contractors." At some point, it dawned on her that she had been attending a lot of funerals of coworkers hit by fast-growing brain cancers and other rare diseases. When she began to feel sick herself, she quit the job and went to work as an accountant for the University of San Francisco. Although her doctor had initially told her the problem was stress, several more months of testing led to a different diagnosis. It turns out that the development she had worked on, spending all those days walking in the dirt, was built on a toxic landfill.

She was diagnosed with lupus, an autoimmune deficiency disease whereby the body attacks itself, and given six months to live. At age thirty-four, Lynn returned home to Birmingham to be close to her family and to fight for her life. To this day, she believes that the community living in the Bay Area development is threatened with "dire harm," as she puts it, but since there is no definitive proof on what causes lupus and there is no way to even identify the potential chemicals that might have been present in the landfill before development began, there is little that she can do to hold the contractors responsible. (Currently under a federal gag order, Lynn is not able to reveal the name of the development or its location.) "Also, right here in Birmingham we manufactured steel," she adds, "so I may have had it all along." Steel production has been linked to lupus by some researchers, and according to Lynn, Birmingham once had one of the highest rates of incidents of the disease in the world.

Nevertheless, she is not the type of person who sits well knowing that she could have done more to help families and children. "You know, that's one of the things that I still think about, I guess because of guilt. I failed to look at what had happened to that community. I just sort of ran with my life. Lynn Battle wasn't supposed to live past 1990. I first met her twelve years later, in 2002.

* * *

I had gone to Anniston, Alabama, to report on a class-action lawsuit against the chemical company Monsanto (makers of saccharin, acrylic, fertilizers, dioxin, and Agent Orange), a company that had polluted Anniston's soil and water with polychlorinated biphenyls (PCBs) from the 1930s to the 1970s. A few years earlier, when Lynn had discovered what was happening in Anniston, she contacted Connie Tucker of the Southern Organizing Committee, who in turn pulled in the attorney Grover Hankins of the Environmental Justice Law Clinic at Texas Southern University.

It wasn't that they were the only citizens taking action, but Lynn was an integral limb on the collective body. Together, the efforts of Tucker, Hankins, and dozens of residents resulted in an early complaint based on the testimony of six key plaintiffs. She was the kind of person who could get the ball rolling and make things happen. She knew how to pick up a phone and "beg and cry" as she likes to say, for whatever was needed: computers, money, legal aid, housing, furniture, transportation, votes.

By 2003, the Anniston case (much mutated and strained with the involvement of some twenty-eight lawyers including Johnnie Cochran) would result in a monumental settlement of $750 million for over eighteen thousand plaintiffs to be paid by Monsanto and its holdings, Solutia, Pfizer, and Pharmacia. It was the largest class-action settlement ever won against an environmental polluter in America. The company knew it was liable, of course, long before the case ever went to court. "PCBs cannot be considered nontoxic," stated an internal memo as early as 1935. They knew that in 1966, fish dropped into the creek near the plant "turned belly-up within seconds, spurting blood and shedding skin." "Direct lawsuits are possible," warned another 1969 Monsanto memo.

Lynn's anger at such deception had been brewing for some time, as she began to connect the dots between her own illness and so many diseases in working-class and poor communities of color. The environmental justice movement has always been led by women just like her, explains Robert Bullard, author of the classic 1990 study *Dumping in Dixie*. They are often retired women of color, schoolteachers or health care workers who operate within tiny, grassroots, mostly volunteer organizations. They receive little, if any, public recognition or financial support for their efforts.

Lynn does not receive a paycheck for her current work as founder and executive director of the Citizens' Lead Education and Poisoning Prevention Program or CLEPP, a small nonprofit organization that receives local government and private funding for subcontracting work in prevention, residential testing and education about the hazards of lead. Instead, she and her daughter survive on income "technically below the poverty line," she says: a small pension from the University of San Francisco plus social security.

In fact, it was Robert Bullard's book *Dumping in Dixie* that set off the lightbulb in Lynn's mind so many years ago when she discovered it on the shelf of a Birmingham public library. She had only recently returned to Birmingham, and was at home on disability. The book jumped out at her. "Especially that sentence," she recalls, "where he says, 'Try to think of a black community that's not bordered by a railroad track, freeway, or factory.' It opened my mind and made me really angry," she says. "We thought we were going through something isolated. It never occurred to us that this was happening all over the county."

Not long after reading Bullard's book, Lynn waged war against Browning-Ferris Industries (BFI), a waste-management company that tried unsuccessfully to install a toxic dump in the largely black community of North Titusville, Alabama. She became aware of the company's plans when they showed up at a neighborhood association meeting to announce that they were moving in. "Interesting fight," she recalls with typical understatement. In reality, she is what folks at the Environmental Protection Agency call a "worthy adversary." "She has balls of steel," according to one local legislator.

Lynn and other community advocates forced Browning-Ferris to take their garbage elsewhere.

But of all the deadly toxins Americans are exposed to everyday, lead poisoning is the problem closest to Lynn's heart, because of its harsh impact on children. Black children have blood levels that are 80 percent higher than those of white children in this country. To put it another way, African Americans are at five times the risk than whites, and poor children of all races are eight times more likely to be exposed. The problem of lead also has personal meaning for Lynn.

When her daughter Destiny was a toddler, her pediatrician prescribed calcium supplements to help heal the bones of a broken leg. Nine months later, Destiny was diagnosed with elevated blood lead levels. It didn't take much research for Lynn to discover that calcium supplements are made from the ground bones of animals and oyster shells and that these contain lead. Destiny, who is now eleven, was lucky. Low levels of lead, if found while still in the blood, can be flushed out of the body with a diet rich in calcium, iron, and green, leafy vegetables.

And yet, although she seems fine today, Destiny continues to have difficulty with writing and shows signs of dyslexia. Also, she doesn't understand the concept of rhyming and is unable to compose even basic rhymed sentences. Symptoms of lead poisoning vary widely and it is often difficult to pinpoint the root causes of learning disabilities. Instead, Lynn will always be left to wonder why Destiny has been stunted in this area. Which chemical or toxin is responsible? And from where? "Our home was tested and there was no lead," she says. "But there is lead in calcium supplements. It says so right on the FDA's Web site." Two months after her daughter's diagnosis, she launched the Citizens' Lead Education and Poisoning Prevention Program (CLEPP).

* * *

When I first met Lynn in 2002, early one morning for coffee at the Birmingham Hilton Hotel, she approached with a pigeon-toed limp (three hip replacements and "other things") that gave her compact, powerful frame a quick up-down movement as it swayed from left to right. At forty-seven, her smooth, dark-brown skin was wrinkle-free and she wore her hair in thick, shoulder-length dreadlocks. After just a few minutes with her, one thing about Lynn Battle became clear to me: Her brain moves like a bullet train, already at the station before you've even heard it coming. She seems to be calculating rescue plans, managing her opponents, and slinging wry, stinging witticisms all at once.

"Lead is everywhere," she told me, spreading cream cheese over a slice of bagel. "People come from third-world countries and they bring dishes that we sell it at the 99-cent store . . . coffee cups . . . candles have wicks that were dipped in lead . . . refrigerator magnets and keys that kids play with . . . batteries, old computers." Most importantly, she explained, lead was used in household paint not so long ago, and remains in the majority of all American homes built before 1980. As late as 1980, in fact, an astonishing 88 percent of all American children were lead-poisoned, according to the Centers for Disease Control and Prevention. They are now adults in their twenties and early thirties living and working with who-knows-what effect on their behavior and critical analytical skills.

After World War II, surplus lead paint was mandated for use in government-funded public housing, where it remained prevalent. Herb Needleman, Professor of Pediatrics and Child Psychology at the University of Pittsburgh Medical Center, was an early researcher (the "godfather of lead") hired by the government to study the public health impact of the heavy metal. Uncomfortable with the dire results of his studies, the government fired Needleman and attempted to discredit his findings. "The story of lead paint," write Columbia University professors Gerald Markowitz and David Rosner in their book *Deceit and Denial: The Deadly Politics of Industrial Pollution,* "is that of a guerrilla war fought by small groups of individuals against giant lead corporations."

Lynn Battle is one of those individuals.

Lead still contaminates our air, soil, and water. It resides in our bones, blood, fatty tissues, and organs. Even by conservative estimates, 5 percent of all American children have dangerously high levels. (The Centers for Disease Control maintains that the number is 2 percent and declining.) It may be difficult to foresee the health hazards of more recent creations like PCBs, but the dangers of lead have been known since the days of the Roman Empire, when Nero was poisoned by it. We know that among children under the age of six, it only takes a speck the size of a sugar grain to cause learning and behavioral problems, stunted growth, aggression, antisocial behavior, hyperactivity, attention deficit disorder, memory and hearing loss, poor attention spans, and lowered IQ.

"But since kids aren't foaming at the mouth," says Lynn, "parents don't see it as a big deal. It's invisible and therefore we think it doesn't impact us. The fact that they're coughing, well, say the parents, 'They must not have worn a sweater.'"

It works like this.

Iron is critical for the development of the brain, but since the body can't tell the difference between lead and iron, a growing child "sucks up lead" instead, especially if she doesn't have enough iron in her system to begin with. The frontal lobe, the center of our emotional responses, appears to be most affected by this. "That's the part of the brain that tells us, 'Don't do this or that,'" says Lynn. "That's why you find lead-poisoned kids ending up in special education and prison." (Needleman also argues for a strong connection between criminality, aggression, and lead-poisoned youth.)

Children are most vulnerable to lead because they breathe in more air than adults, eat more food in proportion to their size, and ingest larger amounts of chemicals than their small bodies can process. Their food is mostly milk, which has a high fat content, and toxins are most easily stored in fatty tissues, like breasts. Children also touch their hands to their mouths as many as nine times an hour. Lead dust found in peeling paint is sweet to the taste and can quickly become addictive to infants and toddlers.

The simplest way to prevent lead poisoning would be to remove children from dangerous conditions inside their homes, such as peeling paint and mold. In the spring of 2005, a University of Arizona researcher called the relationship between lead and low academic test scores among schoolchildren "so extreme it's almost beyond belief." And yet,

CLEPP, Lynn Battle's advocacy group, is forced to scrape and claw to help the children of Birmingham; fighting tooth and nail for every penny of funding while meeting with resistance from local and state health and housing authorities, federal officials, members of the public health community, and even private physicians.

"I remember one of the first meetings Lynn had with the Jefferson County Health Department," recalls her friend Max Weintraub, a toxics expert with the PCB division of the Environmental Protection Agency (EPA) in San Francisco. "It was within the first six months of her becoming involved with lead and we were all sitting around a table. She was challenging them about screening children, asking about follow-up and home visits. She was very forceful," says Weintraub, who formerly worked with the National Lead Information Center in Washington, D.C. "It was not a message that was well-received."

In fact, only five states—New York, Massachusetts, New Jersey, Rhode Island, and Illinois—currently require school-age children to be tested for lead for enrollment in public schools, and Alabama is not one of them. But as Don Ryan, founder and former director of the Alliance for Healthy Homes in Washington, D.C., the nation's primary advocacy group for lead-poisoned children notes, even those states have only a 50 to 80 percent success rate in carrying out such testing. In other states, testing is required only for Medicaid children, according to federal guidelines, and their success rate is less than 20 percent, an abysmal performance. A 2005 University of Michigan study agreed, finding that only about half of lead-poisoned Medicaid children receive any kind of follow-up at all.

When Lynn challenged Birmingham health officials on the issue of testing, says Max Weintraub, "it just got quieter and quieter in the room. She sort of chastised them. The attacks weren't personal. It was just to say, 'The Department of Housing and Urban Development (HUD) has millions of dollars to help you with this, so why hasn't anyone applied for the funds?'"

Eventually, Jefferson County did apply for, and receive, federal lead abatement money. "Only because Lynn shamed them into it," says Weintraub. "Before her, there just wasn't a high level of awareness or political push behind eliminating lead poisoning. Lynn made it happen in Birmingham.

"Alabama is a beautiful state in the springtime," she tells me, pointing out the early-blooming yellow forsythias. "Our ancestors fought for this place with their labor," she says, "and I'm not going to give it up."

Admittedly, some of her tactics have been bold.

Like the time she loaded a group of lead-poisoned, hyperactive children onto a bus and delivered them to the offices of state legislators in Montgomery. It was one of her more provocative moves. She doesn't give details of what happened, saying only, "That was fun."

Legislators must have hated you, I offer.

"Yeah," she agrees. "But we got the lead law passed."

* * *

One spring afternoon, I rode with Lynn and two CLEPP staffers to a Birmingham suburb to visit the white, middle-class family of a nineteen-month-old boy named Alex. Lynn wanted me to meet Alex to make it clear that white children are harmed by lead, too. Often, "the only difference between a lead-poisoned child and one diagnosed with Attention Deficit and Hyperactivity Disorder (the most commonly diagnosed behavioral disorder among children) is economics and race."

Children like Alex live not in urban housing projects, but in modest, middle-class, white communities, and even ocean-side mansions along the coasts of states like Rhode Island and Massachusetts, where lead levels are extremely high and saltwater contributes to the rapid deterioration of paint. When these middle- and upper-income families decide to renovate their homes and knock down walls, they unwittingly expose their children to lead.

Alex suffered for months from severe stomach cramps and a poor appetite. He was hyperactive and his screaming and crying were incessant. His private family doctor did not consider lead, however, and simply assumed that Alex had a bad case of the terrible twos. Alex's parents were persistent, and for months they made frantic phone calls to health officials and medical professionals, seeking further testing. At one point, Alex's distraught father called every office in the phone book with the word "county" in it. When they reached someone with the County Housing Department, authorities suggested that the family contact CLEPP.

From there, Lynn was on the case.

After visiting the family she filed a formal complaint with the Centers for Disease Control contending that the Jefferson County Health Department had tested Alex and then refused to disclose his results to the family. "County officials are required to follow-up on children who test above fifteen," she explained. "But they follow-up just like they followed up Alex. They're never heard from again."

In response to her complaint, the CDC contacted the State Health Department, who then contacted the County office, and Alex's parents were finally given their son's results: Alex's blood level was in the lethal range, at fifty-six micrograms of lead per deciliter of blood. To put that number into perspective, the CDC's "number of concern" is ten micrograms of lead per deciliter of blood, an amount known to decrease a child's I.Q. by as many as three points. (Most experts now agree that even one microgram of lead can cause damage and that there is no safe level of exposure.)

The highest blood lead level Lynn had ever seen was that of Denzel Covington, who she calls her "miracle baby," several years earlier, who tested at sixty-two and had to endure painful chelation therapy at the age of two. Today, Denzel is a healthy seven-year-old boy on the honor roll at his elementary school. This gives Lynn hope that Alex will recover.

"Now I gotta go cry to the County Commissioner for some money to fix their house," she tells me as we pile back into her car. "Hit up a couple of Serta companies for some clean mattresses."

The work of finding safe housing for children falls squarely into the hands of CLEPP because there is no one else. Without it, Birmingham families without knowledge of how the various government agencies work would simply fall through the cracks. "Lead is the stepchild that nobody wants to deal with," she explains. "It throws doctors into a realm that they have no control over. Once they have a child who tests positive, who's going to go out and test the house?" she asks. "Who's going to move the family? There's a social work element to it and a housing element, and by then doctors have bitten off more than they want to chew. Most of them just hide under the covers. I've been saying that substandard housing *is* a medical condition," she adds, enunciating her words for emphasis: *"It is a public health issue."* David Jacobs, former director of the Office of Lead Hazard Control in Housing and Urban Development (HUD) in Washington, D.C., agrees, noting that "lead is a public health problem manifested as a housing problem, which makes it a policy nightmare."

Later that afternoon, we rode to the home of twenty-one-year-old Latoya Counts. There was a Chevy truck parked in the dirt lot outside with a red, white, and blue "God Bless the U.S.A." bumper sticker, and Latoya, who wore her McDonald's uniform, was inside preparing to go to work. The young African American mother was raising two children in the home, along with her sister, who had four children of her own. A ten-year-old nephew was there as well, playing Pac-Man after being suspended from school for fighting. Since aggression is a symptom of lead poisoning, I wondered aloud if the boy had been tested. "He's too old," explained Lynn. "Testing is only done through the age of six. After that, children "disappear from the system" since doctors assume that lead is already stored in the bones and the damage is done.

As with Alex's parents, a predatory lender had sold the century-old home to Latoya and her sister illegally, without offering full disclosure of its lead hazards. When Lynn discovered that the women were paying an astonishing $62,000 mortgage and astronomical interest rates her voice escalated from low, controlled tones to high-pitched decibels. At a certain point she was virtually squeaking. "They could have bought a brand-new home in Birmingham for $80,000!" she said. "Now they gotta raise those children in that crap!"

* * *

In 2000, HUD, the EPA, and the CDC announced that they would work together to eliminate lead poisoning by the year 2010. But it is difficult to take promises of reform seriously when the EPA's own Web site offers a lead history timeline that inexplicably ends in 1988, with the decline of leaded gasoline, and makes no mention of present-day problems. Most recently, the Bush administration even took a pass on imposing mandatory regulations for home and commercial improvements, where lead is most likely to be kicked up during renovations. The administration is also proposing a decrease in 2006 funding for the one agency within HUD that has successfully addressed the problem of lead: the Office of Lead Hazard Control. "It doesn't make sense," says former director David Jacobs. "This was one of the few well-run programs within HUD that was actually working."

It will be very difficult, as Don Ryan of the Alliance for Healthy Homes warns, "to do justice to all the different dimensions of lead in one chapter." The problem, he says, extends "from the health system's failure to screen children, to the Medicaid connection, to landlords, courts, and local and state agencies who are supposed to enforce codes, to discrimination and predators, and equity questions involving federal funding for low-income housing. It's like sewing without a knot in the thread." In fact, I spoke with Ryan in the spring of 2005 as he was packing up his office, preparing to retire from his organization after fifteen years of advocacy for lead-poisoned children. When asked why he was leaving, he said simply, "Burnout." Lead in the average population is down 90 percent, he noted, "but the job is far from done. And what remains of lead disproportionately affects the poor and minorities."

By June of 2005, Lynn, too, was becoming weary with the effects of burnout as well as renewed health complications due to the lupus and a diagnosis of multiple sclerosis. The number of staffers at CLEPP was down to four and Lynn was mostly working from home. Her organization was moved to an abandoned elementary school inside the Tuxedo Housing Projects, where it had been absorbed by the Jefferson County Committee for Economic Opportunity.

The term "environmental racism" was coined in 1982 to describe large-scale toxic dumping nationwide in mostly low-income communities of color. Poor and working-class black women are at the forefront of local movements against such dumping, as they struggle to protect their families. But they cannot fight the giants alone.

"We've turned into a right-now society," says Lynn, "where if I produce this product I'm getting my money right now. And a lot of people assume that the government is protecting us, but it isn't. We have beautiful sunsets," she continues looking out into a fuzzy Birmingham horizon. ". . . purple and orange . . . but that's pollution. People are going to have to start making connections."

"I've turned it into a board game," she says of her fight against lead and other toxins. "Some days I'm winning. Some days I'm losing. But I'm still somewhere on the board," she adds. "I'm still on the board."

In November of 2005, Lynn announced that the office of CLEPP would be closing its doors due to her own declining health.

5.

Yvonne Sanders at age 14 in her hometown of Greenwood, Mississippi.

TEACHER

Lithonia, Georgia

W hen Yvonne Sanders-Butler talks about the decision to change her life nearly a decade ago, she speaks slowly and deliberately with a heavy Southern drawl that somehow sounds lighter here, in her presence, than it does on my tape recorder later. She has soft, feminine features and wide, watery brown eyes, and seems even smaller than her petite five feet four when she is curled up on a leather couch in her ranch home in Ellenwood, Georgia. Here, the ambitions of the nationally acclaimed elementary school principal, cookbook author, and entrepreneur who is always prepared with a press kit and a sound bite soften somewhat as she presents herself without makeup, wearing a head scarf and house slippers. She shares this space with her twenty-one-year-old son Denard, a rodeo calf roper who is away for the weekend at a competition, and her husband Floyd, a welding engineer and prize horse trainer who positions one arm protectively across the couch behind his wife as she speaks.

"I was always a dieter," says Yvonne. "And everyone in my family was concerned about my weight. Either I would eat certain things and just want to sleep and not be bothered," she says. "Or I would get hyped up and anxious and it had to happen right now, I wanted it *right now*. I can be very aggressive when I want something," she admits. "And even I didn't realize how off-the-wall I could be." There were days, she says, when she would just drink coffee and take diet pills. "Floyd and Denard would stay outside with the horses, so relaxed . . . And I would watch them and not understand why I was so angry and frustrated. Just pulsating all the time."

"We tried to get her into the horses," says Floyd, "to calm her down." But that didn't work. "I was always in school with things to do" says Yvonne, "and they were so much better at it than I was. I would get frustrated."

Yvonne's six sisters, all college-educated and informed about good nutrition (one is a physician) were different. They were relatively slim and understood the concept of moderation in diet. Dorothy Sanders-Walls, a paralegal in Greenville,

Mississippi, who is ten years Yvonne's senior, had always eaten a healthy, mostly vegetable-based diet ("sunflower seeds instead of potato chips") and when visiting her older sister during the summers, even the chubby child would lose weight. But what neither Yvonne nor her family fully understood at the time was that food held a much deeper meaning for her.

Born and raised in a tiny, wooden-framed farmhouse without indoor plumbing in the cotton fields of Vons, Mississippi, Yvonne grew up, as she says, "surrounded by love. There were men in my family who were mechanics and farmers and whisky makers and good fathers," she recalls wistfully, who brought home sugarcane from the Louisiana fields for a young girl's Christmas treat. Men like Uncle Shephard, who was mildly mentally retarded and who walked two miles from the cotton gin to her schoolhouse to bring her a bag of candy, and taught who her about the changing seasons and wildlife. And there were women who baked and scrubbed and kept her cozy home filled with home-cooked meals. Women like Miss Earline, her "second mother," who "gave picking cotton dignity in 105-degree weather" as Yvonne would later write in one of her three cookbooks. Miss Earline brought dinner to the fields: chilled buttermilk and hot chicken; molasses bread in large tin pans wrapped in white towels.

In fact, Yvonne's memories of food were deeply tied to a mother's love. Ruth Sanders had thrived in her kitchen. From

Yvonne's perspective, it was the place that most filled her mother with a sense of peace and security. It was where she canned her own fruits and vegetables and cooked in a large black potbelly stove, desserts so special that children weren't allowed to "walk hard" on the floor while they were baking. Ruth sat Yvonne on a tree stump beside her in the kitchen when her daughter was just three, and taught her everything she knew. Even today, Yvonne's voice turns dreamy when she recalls growing up in her mother's kitchen, helping her to stir batter.

The traditional farming diet was a good one, she says, calling it the model we need to return to. "Every autumn the men would kill a hog. We'd cure it, put it in the storehouse, and use the salt meat to flavor vegetables." There wasn't a lot of fried food or meat because the family couldn't afford it. Instead, there were "pinto and lima and green beans from the gardens almost every day . . . turnips and cabbage, collards and mustards . . . and fruit orchards teeming with watermelon and cantaloupe."

"Yvonne was always hanging around the kitchen," recalls her sister Dorothy. "She was mama's little helper. I think she really preferred cooking even to playing." But as with any addiction, there is usually a rock bottom.

Yvonne's came the night she was rushed to the hospital on the verge of a massive stroke, at the age of thirty-six. She was diagnosed with hypertension and sarcoidosis, a lupus-related disease causing severe arthritis symptoms. Her doctor told her that she needed to lose fifty pounds to take the pressure off her severely weakened joints. Yvonne's sister Betty suggested Overeaters Anonymous.

"I was a strong black female with several degrees," says Yvonne. "I did not see myself as someone who needed a support group." But even with her Bachelor of Science from Jackson State University, her Specialist Degree in Counseling from the State University of West Georgia, and her recent acceptance into a doctoral program in Educational Leadership at Florida's Sarasota University, she knew, deep down, that she wasn't happy. Overeaters Anonymous helped her to look inside, at what was really going on in her heart. She was married to her childhood sweetheart, the man she had loved since grade school; she was wearing designer clothes, joking and laughing and presenting an image of success to the world. "People thought I was a go-getter," she says. But inside, her self-esteem "was not quite where it should have been." The private Yvonne that her family lived with was "a shell of a woman," she says. "Just drugged up on food."

At Overeaters Anonymous, Yvonne felt that she could finally let down her guard and show her weaknesses. When she announced to Floyd that she was cutting out all added sugars from her diet, he was skeptical at first. "You go on more diets than Oprah," he replied. It was true. Only this time Yvonne had made a major breakthrough. She realized that it wasn't about a diet. It was about a lifestyle change.

"She started researching," recalls Dorothy, "and when she came back from Overeaters Anonymous she said that she was going to change some things. I saw her the following Thanksgiving and she had gone down ten dress sizes."

"In college Yvonne would start a lot of projects but would never complete anything," explains Floyd. There were various business ventures from thrift stores to making bears, gift baskets and flowers. "I would get bored and impatient with everything," says Yvonne, who has also been diagnosed with attention deficit disorder. With the change in her diet, however, Floyd began to see a major difference. "She could actually sit and complete a task. Her concentration was better and she could stay focused." Before long, Yvonne had Floyd and Denard off the "cookies, cakes, ice cream, junk food, fast food" too, and Denard was thriving as an aspiring athlete. Over a period of six months, Yvonne's weight fell from 190 to 140 pounds, where it has remained for the past eight years at a comfortable size six.

"She surprised us," says Dorothy. "I never would have imagined."

* * *

By 1998, two years after she had been rushed to the hospital, Yvonne Butler had completed her doctorate and was hired as school principal of Browns Mill Elementary Arts and Magnet School in Lithonia, Georgia.

Immediately, she noticed that something was wrong at the school. Students were showing up at the nurse's office before the day had even begun, complaining of fatigue, headaches, and stomachaches. An increasing number also had disciplinary problems, and many were taking medication for hyperactivity, asthma, and diabetes. "The kindergarteners were so big that they looked like second graders . . . They threw nearly all their vegetables and fruits away and swapped lunch items with the skill of Wall Street stockbrokers . . . And they didn't drink water at all." Yvonne knew all about it. As a child, she had even shot marbles with other kids in an effort to win their cookies and milk. Now that she had made the connection between her own poor diet and chaotic state-of-mind, she realized that something had to be done to help the children.

Located in DeKalb County, the second most affluent African American community in the country, Browns Mill students were being groomed for prestigious black colleges like Howard and Morehouse and professional, white-collar careers. Their parents were "politically active and educated," says Yvonne, with college degrees and Internet access. And the public school was one of only a handful in the country with a revolutionary arts-based educational focus on music, fine arts, and theater. (In fact, when I visited, third-graders learned about Romare Bearden, the blues, and the Great Migration, all in one action-packed audio and visually enhanced lesson.) Clearly, these kids were being primed for the extraordinary. They were privileged, talented. And yet, they were testing as though they were from disintegrating communities, with academic scores below the national average. The pieces didn't fit.

And so, in the fall of 1999, one year after becoming principal, Yvonne Butler made a monumental decision. She eliminated all processed foods from the cafeteria, as well as foods with added sugars and high fat. In short, she made Browns Mill the first sugar-free school in America. And she didn't stop there.

Yvonne also prohibited foods with added sugars on school grounds, in staff rooms, and sack lunches brought from home. And in actions that would later be mirrored by other schools across the nation, she renegotiated a contract with Coca-Cola to replace soda in vending machines with Dasani bottled water. At local grocery stores, she convinced merchants to replace candy with healthy snacks in their most prominent displays: graham crackers, rice cakes, granola bars, soy milk, and convenient lunchbox-sized bottled water. For her teachers and staff, Yvonne secured a $5,000 grant from the DeKalb County Health Department to buy commercial treadmills, yoga and Pilates mats, and free weights for the gym, to be used during staff-only hours. She instituted cooking classes and twelve-step support groups for parents, students, and teachers, including lessons in meal preparation and how to read food labels. She hit the pavement at school-board meetings and in shopping malls, spreading the word to potential corporate sponsors, many of whom have since pledged funding to help Browns Mill's battle with obesity.

Decreasing added sugars should hardly be considered a revolutionary idea.

In 2003, the World Health Organization and the United Nations Food and Agriculture Organization released a routine report recommending a 10 percent limit on "free sugars" in common foods like peanut butter and mayonnaise (foods that don't need sugar to begin with). Such campaigns are becoming more and more common across the country, and there is evidence that they work. That same year, Northwestern University Medical School researchers implemented an anti-obesity program at Chicago's Head Start where teachers used puppets like "Miss Grain," "Mr. Protein," "Mr. Fat," and "Miss Sugar" to educate children about the importance of exercise and healthy diets. Two years later, the youth who participated in the program were slimmer than those who had not, according to the *Chicago Sun Daily Times.*

But seven years ago, when Yvonne Butler began her program, the nation was not yet in an uproar about obesity among children and the Browns Mill plan was just strange enough to be considered controversial. Many parents were outraged by the "sugar-free zone," which they saw as extreme.

Elaine Archie-Booker, Ph.D. is both a member of the school counsel and an Adjunct Assistant Professor in Community Health and Preventative Medicine at Morehouse College. And yet, even she initially resisted the sugar-free program. "I had to understand what it was about," Elaine explained to me when I asked how someone with her professional training could oppose a sugar-free school. "These kids are used to having birthday parties with cupcakes and cookies . . . and coming from an atmosphere of having all the sugar you want takes a transition." She was also skeptical of the plan, she admitted, simply because she didn't understand the changes that she and her daughter were being subjected to, or why they were necessary. "My thing was 'What do you mean by sugar free? What are we talking about?' Because not many people really sit down and take a course on how to read labels. Most ordinary people wouldn't know about that."

So Yvonne explained to them exactly what she meant.

"We know that *natural* sugars already present in foods such as milk and fruit and that's fine. We're just trying to get rid of *added* sugars in foods like chocolate milk, pancake syrup, and high fructose punch." Natural sugars, she explained, are those that are not enriched, bleached or processed such as sugarcane, turbinado, organic maple, unsulphured molasses, and fruit juices. "It's like the difference between coke and crack" in that refined sugars take effect far more quickly and are more addictive. She argues that we can, in fact, control sugar cravings, digestive problems, and unnecessary weight gain simply by substituting key ingredients in our recipes. Unbleached or soy flour, for example, retains vitamins and minerals and provides fiber without chemicals. Soy is an excellent substitute for dairy because it decreases saturated fatty acids. Similarly, the eggs she buys are from organic free-range hens only, raised without hormones or pesticides. The key to a healthy diet, she says, is balance.

It's okay if a meal has lots of starches like potato salad or macaroni and cheese, she writes in her cookbook *Naturally Yours Gourmet Desserts*. But then "why not serve a light dessert . . . like a nice, light soy ice cream with fresh fruit" to go with it? "If, on the other hand, what you really want is a rich chocolate cake for dessert, then prepare lots of cooked and raw, leafy green vegetables to go with your meal." On holidays when you plan to eat a lot of rich foods, she advises, begin the morning with "warm lemon water along with a grapefruit or other citrus fruit" to help "cleanse and revitalize the body." (Her second and third books *Dessert Lovers' Choice: Naturally Sweet, Naturally Delicious* and *Healthy Kids, Smart Kids: The Principal-Created, Parent-Tested, Kid-Approved Nutrition Plan for Sound Bodies and Strong Minds* were released in September of 2005.)

It's all about reconditioning the mind and the taste buds, explained Yvonne to parents and staff. "A lot of people want to lose twenty pounds and be healthier, but they don't know what to do. So they do everything, going 'round and 'round in circles. That's the hardest part," she says. "People are afraid of what they don't know. They're afraid of failure." But you *can* learn to reprogram old eating habits. Yvonne taught by example. "I used to sweeten everything. Now, if I get a hit of regular sugar [and regular sugar does include brown sugar and honey] I'm out of it. It's like I've had four glasses of wine. I can't do anything."

For Elaine Booker, this way of thinking challenged her typical routine of "rippin' and running." Mornings for the busy professional and single mother had always consisted of coffee, no food. Lunch and dinner were on the go as well. "I had to learn to slow down," she admits today. Now, breakfast for her and her daughter is usually oatmeal and fruit. She makes a conscious effort to prepare menus, making sure that she keeps nuts in the car and stocks up on healthy snacks like yogurt and grapes. "You can still have your to-go food," she says. "But now it's the *right* to-go food."

In another difficult exchange, Yvonne met with parents who were enraged that a teacher had taken away their son's cake at lunchtime. "This piece of red velvet cake," recalls Yvonne, "could have served three children. It was huge. And the boy was already overweight." No matter what the size, it was prohibited according to Browns Mill regulations, so the teacher stored the cake (it would be returned at the end of the day) and gave the student a piece of fruit instead. The parents, both whom were school teachers themselves, took it personally, recalls Yvonne. "I was really sort of challenged on that one." But she stood her ground. "The rules of Browns Mill are in the handbook," she said. "This is a sugar-free zone."

And then she turned on the charm.

"I said: 'Look guys, you're here because you want the best education for your child. But what will it matter if their lifespan is shortened? I'm a busy mom too and I understand what it means to be doing the best you can. So you swing into a fast food restaurant and you pick up some stuff so the child can have a breakfast, right? But instead of fueling the child for the day, you've just set him up for failure. I don't want anything less for your child than I want for my own son," she added. "And you just can't put regular gas in a Mercedes. I consider *every* child a Mercedes."

Today, thanks to a comprehensive dietary education, it is the students themselves who do much of the monitoring of meals at Browns Mill. Diplomatic officers for each grade level wear special vests and walk the cafeteria rows keeping an eye on the food kids bring from home, and most students themselves remind parents not to pack certain items in their lunches. Student officers also make sure that administrators provide extra water and grapes (vitamin B "brain food") on academic testing days. They are aware now, says Yvonne, and they understand that "certain foods will affect their beautiful skin and their hair won't be as shiny and strong, and they won't grow as tall."

"Kids know when they feel good and when they don't," agrees parent Angela Joyner. Angela and her husband Dorian, who is president of the PTA, were both early supporters of the sugar-free program for their three sons, now fifteen, twelve, and nine. "Even though they may like sugar," says Angela, "they also realize when it makes them feel tired, or anxious and frustrated."

* * *

In 2001, Yvonne's home state of Mississippi became the first in the nation to reach a 25 percent obesity rate. Soon afterward, Georgia surpassed Mississippi with 37 percent of its children and adolescents *alone* tipping the scales too far. Some municipal pockets are even more dramatic. In New York City, for example, 43 percent of elementary school students are overweight and obese. We've all heard the numbers: 65 percent of all Americans are overweight. Even 10 percent of *toddlers* under the age of five are obese today. Recently, scientists pointed out that by the year 2050 our gains in life expectancy will reverse themselves for the first time in decades due to the "epidemic of obesity" among children, which has tripled since 1975.

Among African Americans these numbers are even more staggering.

More than 80 percent of black women over the age of forty are overweight and 50 percent of these are obese. Like Yvonne's mother, Ruth Sanders, who died in 2003 of liver cancer, African Americans are 23 percent more likely to die from cancer than whites. Like Yvonne's uncle Shephard and Miss Earline, we are twice as likely to have diabetes and cardiovascular disease. And like Yvonne herself, black Americans have the highest rates of hypertension than any other racial group in the country. Like Yvonne, they are also less likely to be aware of the warning signs of a stroke than non-blacks, and are therefore more likely to die from such attacks.

There are many reasons for the increase in obesity in America. Here are just a few: the corn syrup industry has seen a fivefold increase in sales and production in the past three decades; the soft drink industry now provides the single greatest source of refined sugar in the American diet with the average person drinking over six hundred cans a year; and the fast food industry is booming. All told, the average American now consumes about two pounds of sugar per week. In addition, sedentary lifestyles mean that we spend on average, about five hours a day in front of a television set. Just two hours of television a day have been found to increase the risk of childhood obesity by 23 percent. African Americans watch, on average, 50 percent more television than the general population and the children of Browns Mill Elementary Arts and Magnet School are no different.

But at least now they have a fighting chance. After just one sugar-free semester at Browns Mill, the number of students seeking the nurse's aid in the morning hours fell by 30 percent. The school also saw a steady decline in referrals for discipline and counseling. When I visited the cafeteria there, in the winter of 2004, I found head cook Valerie Johnson laying out a gorgeous display of pineapple slices, green and orange melon chunks, whole strawberries, and red grapes. For breakfast, students had oatmeal, turkey sausage, fruit, and all-natural juices. For lunch, there was baked chicken, green beans and whole-wheat biscuits.

In the hallways, a plethora of posters advertised constant messages about nutrition and diet. One collage made by students included cardboard cut-outs of carrots, oranges, pears, peas, and celery sticks pasted onto the image of a computer that read,. "Program your brain for healthy eating." Staff members spun by with pedometers clipped onto their waistbands. (They were in competition for a trip to Las Vegas to be given to the team with the most monthly steps.)

Similarly, children at Browns Mill struck me as bright-eyed and energetic. When asked their favorite vegetable, a room of fifth-grade hands shot into the air: "Ooooooh! Corn!" cried one. "Broccoli!" shouted another. "Carrots," said a third. "And why do you like fruits and vegetables?" asked their teacher. "Because they're healthy." "Because they give you strong bones." "Because they're good for you."

Of course, not all of them bought into the sugar-free agenda. "I like McDonald's French fries," one girl told me when I asked her favorite food. Another was a fan of iced tea with lots of sugar. She didn't care for the drinks at school, she added, because "they don't have no flavor." I thought of them later, when I passed a group of high school kids in a McDonald's parking lot smoking cigarettes. The choice would always be theirs. And the students weren't the only ones wrestling with difficult choices.

"When I came to Browns Mill," Assistant Principal Hazel A. Lucas told me, "I was wearing a size twenty-two." Yvonne invited her to an Overeaters Anonymous meeting. "I said I'm too busy," recalled Hazel. "I work, my children are in school, I pick them up from football and cheerleading, and then I go to church and I have a headache all the time and I just can't go to another meeting. I said, 'I'm tired. I can't do it.'"

The truth was Hazel was still in denial about her unhealthy lifestyle. "I figured I didn't eat seconds or thirds. You know how people wake up in the middle of the night and go get a sandwich?" she said. "Well, I have *never* done that." In fact, her diet consisted of fast food, hamburgers, and French fries, and she knew it.

At her first Overeaters Anonymous meeting, she listened as one woman described losing ninety-four pounds. "Somebody else said seventy-six pounds. Then somebody else said fifty-two pounds. I didn't say anything for weeks," says Hazel. "I just gave my name. But I was steady losing weight. Sometimes I can't believe it myself," she adds, showing me a picture of herself fifty-six pounds heavier. For Hazel, the support of colleagues at Browns Mill has been crucial to her success. "I'm a colon cancer survivor," she says simply. "So I'm *very clear* about the need for this program. We've become a family. And this has become a way of life and a part of us."

School counselor Dr. Tanyetta Goodjiones agrees. Growing up Muslim in her mother's home, she was raised without pork and very little sugar. On her father's side of the family, however, there were very different eating habits and relatives who suffered from "a lot of obesity and high blood pressure" because of it. "They ate pig's feet and pork," said Tanyetta, with whom I spoke over a homemade lunch made by Yvonne (green salad, whole wheat bread with tuna salad, and potato salad with red onions) in a conference room adjacent to the principal's large, private office. Here, staff members gathered on a daily basis to eat, talk about the changes in their lives, and share their personal and professional challenges.

"I would call my mother in tears," says Tanyetta, "because I couldn't eat the food. My father's family teased us as children, calling us 'picky.' I was just so glad to be here, in an atmosphere where I don't have to hide and eat in another room because people make you feel bad or strange about your choices."

* * *

Although the majority of states have now proposed legislation attempting to restrict or ban the sale of soda in schools, it is still easier to find than fruit on most campuses. One South Carolina school alone has forty-two Pepsi machines netting $41,000 in annual school profits. The money is used to buy computers, football equipment, paper, and other items that the school is unable to pay for itself.

And the battle continues.

In 2004, Georgia State Representative Stephanie Stuckey

Benfield introduced what seemed like reasonable piece of legislation: a bill that would require schools to measure the weight of students and send the results home to parents, along with information about health and nutrition. Similar efforts in Pennsylvania had already contributed to a 2.6 percent drop in that state's obesity, and the BMI program has been instituted in Arkansas as well. But Benfield was shot down. "Pummeled," she told local reporters. Subsequent attempts by both Benfield and Sally Harrell (D-Atlanta) to require recess and physical education classes in Georgia schools have also failed.

New Jersey, on the other hand, won a major victory against obesity in June of 2005 when it became the first state to ban soda, candy, and foods with high sugar content from all schools K–12. (Other states such as New York, Texas, and California have banned such foods in elementary and middle schools only.)

For its part, the Department of Health and Human Services launched an African American Obesity Initiative in April of 2005, pledging $1.2 million to the National Urban League, the National Council for Negro Women, and the National Association for Equal Opportunity in Higher Education.

But when asked why it continues to send foods loaded with sugars (frosted cereals, high fructose juice drinks, and snacks like the "super donut") to schools, the United States Department of Agriculture's response was noncommittal. A spokesperson from the USDA's Office of Community and Government Affairs told me that such "foods are not reviewed for nutritional requirements" but rather for "how they meet food-based meal pattern requirements in terms of fat content, vegetables, and grains." Since items such as the "super donut" have enriched flour and grains and are vitamin C enriched, they meet some of these requirements. When asked why not simply send foods with vitamin C and little or no sugar, the spokesperson acknowledged that some foods are "very high in fat" and it is simply up to individual school districts to "make sure that other foods eaten in combination with these are low in fat." (Yvonne says that even as recently as 2003 the USDA sent her chocolate milk, which her school hasn't used in years, and which she did not ask for.)

"Cafeterias in public schools started trying to compete with Taco Bell and Kentucky Fried Chicken," she explains. At Browns Mill, and hopefully other schools, the plan is to actually cook food "that doesn't come ready-made in a bag or a box loaded with preservatives." Yvonne believes that by the fall of 2006, some of these changes may actually take place as dietary practices that will hopefully face closer scrutiny when public schools K–12 will be required by federal law to have a "wellness policy," according to the Child Nutrition and WIC Reauthorization Act of 2004. Still, the specifics of such policies will be left in the hands of individual districts and local school boards. It does not seem likely to me, given the current cultural climate, that many schools will follow the lead of Browns Mill.

"Mostly we're still marching to our own drum," says Yvonne. "But over nine million children are overweight in this country. There has to be a movement for change, and I want to be a part of it."

6.

A young Rosalie Williams, with her aunt Leona.

FARMER

Bakersfield, Vermont

About two hours north of Burlington, Vermont, not far from the Canadian border, there is a bridge that runs above the main highway. To the west of the highway is a bustling town called St. Albans, a thriving community with movie theaters and bowling alleys, boutiques and restaurants, and a downtown square with trees, park benches, and landscaping meant for cozy Sunday afternoon strolls. There are elegant wine bars and cafés and a variety of churches and schools. To the east, however, at the top of what feels like an endless hillside expanse, is a very different community: a far more rural and isolated town called Bakersfield that is without bowling alleys or restaurants or movie theaters, or much of anything at all.

Although the drive from St. Albans to Bakersfield takes less than thirty minutes, it feels like days, with nothing to see but distant farmhouses and corn bunkers insulated with plastic sheeting and old rubber tires. There is one gas station and mini-market along the way, in Fairfield, a blip of a town whose only claim to fame is that it was the birthplace of Chester A. Arthur, the twenty-first President of the United States who took office after the assassination of James A. Garfield. Other than occasional grazing cows and maple syrup for sale, there is no industry to speak of. Cold Hollow Cider, the once locally famous apple cider business was here, but had to move to Waterbury, near the Ben & Jerry's Ice Cream Factory, when Bakersfield's zoning board wouldn't allow it to expand. With a population of twelve hundred, Bakersfield is home to less than a dozen family farms today—which is why most families commute (complaining all the way) to and from St. Albans for a paycheck.

After making this drive a few times, it occurs to me that the problem here is more about desolation than distance. Geography fuels apathy in this place; the kind that allows parents to leave children home alone with microwaveable frozen dinners, to be eaten on living-room floors in front of television sets. There are youth in town who have never even learned to use a stove. Boredom is rampant and teenage pregnancies are a major problem. Drug rehabilitation centers also figure prominently along the main highway between St. Albans and Bakersfield: marijuana, a preferred recreational activity, is more common than cigarettes in Vermont high schools.

When I arrive in Bakersfield, 49-year-old organic farmer Rosalie Williams, who has lived here all her life, is nervous. She is eager to please, talkative, and bubbling over with a range of emotions. She is alternately joyful, anxious, tearful, frustrated, hopeful, and proud, and sometimes all of the above within the same ten-minute span of conversation. A compact and energetic woman, she moves about quickly, gathering papers and indicating points of interest. Often, she speaks in long, uninterrupted chains of sentences that quickly form paragraphs, and leave her listener feeling both inspired and spent.

The grayish-blue home that Rosalie shares with her husband Clifford and two daughters is next to a Mobil gas station, separated by a low concrete wall where Terah, their eldest daughter, has planted an abundance of flowers and herbs: pansies, daffodils, marigolds, Egyptian walking onions, ganzia, and mint. Daughter Celia lives here too, with her own daughter, Erionah James, a steely blue-eyed two-year-old presence. In 1994, when Terah and Celia were sixteen and nine, and their brother Lucas was fourteen, Rosalie decided to give up her job driving a school bus so that she could spend more time with her family. Clifford, a supervisor at Northwest State Correctional Facility in St. Albans, was away all day and she figured someone should be home with the children. To make this possible, she decided to resurrect her grandfather's family farm, which had been dormant since 1989.

Clifford was skeptical about the idea at first, pointing out, rightly, that beef prices were at rock bottom and farmers were a dying breed. Indeed, across the nation 330 American farmers go out of business every week, according to the national nonprofit advocacy group Farm Aid. In Vermont, where 4 percent of all dairy farms shut down annually, 1999 was an especially bad year for the state, with 7 percent of dairy farms dying, or 123 families having to quit their business. The situation for black farmers is even more dismal, although Rosalie certainly would not have categorized herself that way at the time. African Americans lose farms at nearly three times the rate of whites and today represent less than 1 percent of all farmers in this country.

"I asked him for a five-year trial period, right Clifford?" says Rosalie over her shoulder. Her husband nods agreement. "And promised him that if I couldn't get the business off its feet by 2003, I'd quit."

But quitting, as Clifford well knows, is not in Rosalie's makeup.

Since the Peaked Hill Family Farm had never used drugs or pesticides, she had a profound advantage; becoming a United States Department of Agriculture Certified Organic Farmer came easily. Organic was the one segment of the farming industry that was experiencing an unusually high annual growth rate of 20 percent. By 2003, Rosalie had solidified her business by joining Organic Valley, the only 100 percent farmer-owned cooperative in the country that produces milk, butter, and cream without antibiotics, synthetic hormones, or pesticides.

The Organic Valley Family of Farms milk cartons are blue and white with cartoon images of a large red barn, and a cow grazing in a green meadow. On one side of a half-gallon box, there is a man wearing overalls and waving. On the other, a little blond girl carries wildflowers alongside a river full of presumably healthy fish. The company envisions itself as "stewards of the earth," saviors of soil and rivers and the farming families themselves. Since its founding in 1988 in LaFarge, Wisconsin, when it was called the Coulee Region Organic Produce Pool (CROPP), Organic Valley's revenue has increased tenfold, from $2 million in 1992 to $156 million in 2003. (Even Miranda Hobbs on *Sex and the City* has Organic Valley in her refrigerator.)

But even beyond the success of these figures, I find it interesting that 22 percent of organic farms in America are run primarily by women, according to the Organic Farming Research Foundation, as compared to just 15 percent of conventional farms. Perhaps, offers Rosalie, this is because men have a harder time with change. It's something about their egos, she says, and the fear of failure.

I went to see Rosalie Williams because I wanted to hear her thoughts about rGBH, the controversial artificial growth hormone routinely injected into American cows to increase their milk production. The hormone, which is manufactured by Monsanto and widely believed to be carcinogenic, is banned on European and Canadian dairy farms and shunned in "every other industrialized country on the planet" except ours, according to investigative reporter Jane Akre. In this country however, rGBH remains legal, unlabeled, and present in many of our commercial milk products. That the public remains largely unaware of its potential dangers is no accident.

A four-part investigative report on the topic by the award-winning former husband and wife journalist team of Jane Akre and Steve Wilson was scheduled to air in February of 1997 on WTVT, a local Fox station in Florida, but was killed after Monsanto attorneys made their disapproval known. Akre was later awarded $425,000 for improper termination by a jury that found Fox guilty of pressuring her to present a "false, distorted or slanted news report." The ruling was over-turned in 2003 on appeal and the couple, who remained unemployed for years following their termination, has since divorced.

It was the FDA's approval of rGBH ten years before this case, in 1993, that was largely responsible for the boom in organic sales among skeptical consumers willing and able to pay higher prices for rGBH-free products.

When I first heard about Rosalie Williams—one of the few black female organic farmers in the country—I hoped that she would talk to me about race and the politics of land ownership, especially in the wake of the monumental 1997 civil rights case of *Pigford v. Veneman*, whereby the USDA agreed to compensate black farmers for billions of dollars in lost land, after the government admitted to willfully and systematically denying African Americans crop loans over a period of at least fifteen years. (Despite the settlement, the USDA has so far denied payments to 86 percent of claimants. Advocates are demanding that the case be reopened.)

I had hoped that Rosalie would talk to me about cancer among African Americans, and the links between such illnesses and our diets. I wondered if she might even know something about recent attempts by the Food and Drug Administration (FDA) to inflict unlabeled milk and meat containing hormone additives on shoppers and to add cloned-animal products, including milk, to our grocer's shelves as well.

I wondered if she would be as outraged by these efforts as I was.

But Rosalie Williams didn't quite fit into my plans in the way I expected.

In fact, she wasn't at all conscious about racial politics. She wasn't like black farmers at say, Austin Farmers Market near Chicago, who sell organic greens, turnips, and okra and consider eating "a political act." And she wasn't like the hip-hop People's Grocery in Oakland, California, with its purple and orange solar-powered van, spreading the word about nutrition to urban neighborhoods.

In fact, when I told her that I wrote for *Essence* magazine, it was Clifford who had to explain what the publication was.

I soon discovered that even asking Rosalie about her racial background sent her into flurries of embarrassment and disclaimers. She wasn't sure if she should be described in that way, she told me during our first phone conversation, before I had any inkling that she was fair-skinned. She certainly didn't look white to me, but then again, she had never used words like "African American" to describe herself either. Both her mother and father were white, she explained, as were her paternal grandparents who raised her from the time she was a baby, and her aunt Leona, who became her legal guardian after their deaths. (She never knew her mother's parents but from pictures she thought her grandmother looked "like

Sitting Bull," as she put it.) On rare occasions when the subject of race had been raised in Bakersfield, a population that is 97.86 percent white according to the 2000 Census, Rosalie had referred to herself only reluctantly, as "dark."

"I don't really see color," she told me in our early conversations. "I grew up here and I've always just been . . ." Here she paused for a moment, adding, "Accepted, if that's even the word."

Eventually however, a more complicated story would find its way to the surface, with details emerging only gradually and painfully. Though she was indeed a farmer through and through, I soon realized that Rosalie's spiritual vocation was something altogether different. Rosalie had lessons to offer her community that went beyond the confines of her little barn and thirty cows; lessons about race, forgiveness, and the awesome task of nurturing youth and children. At its core, hers was a story about feeding and faith. Hers was a story about the giving and taking of life itself.

* * *

The following information has never been fully reported by any mainstream United States media outlet.

In November of 2003, ten members of the FDA's Veterinary Medicine Advisory Committee gathered in a ballroom of the

Rockville, Maryland, Double Tree Hotel to consider whether or not the government should declare cloned animal milk and meat safe for human consumption. It was a strange meeting to be having on a Tuesday, given that the FDA had already announced its approval in newspaper headlines the previous Friday. Odder still was that cloning industry leader Cyagra provided the bulk of "scientific data" for the FDA. After several hours of presentations, independent committee members were asked to respond to this question: Had the government "adequately identified the hazards and characterized the risks related to food consumption of cloned animals?"

"Not enough data," said Anne M. Parkhurst, professor of biometry at the University of Nebraska-Lincoln, who often held her head in her hands during the proceedings. "Many of the assumptions presented by the FDA today are very believable," offered Marguerite Pappaioanou, associate director for science and policy at the Centers for Disease Control and Prevention. "But I didn't see where the data supported them." Pappaioanou and other committee members wanted the FDA to look more closely at the possibility of increased allergic reactions to milk, the problem of intestinal flora in cloned animals, and the fact that cloned animals suffer increased liver problems and a higher mortality rate.

And yet, stunningly, a *Washington Post* headline following this meeting read: "FDA Panel Backs Cloning in Agriculture."

(The *New York Times* offered a more accurate "Panel Doubts Finding on Cloned-Food Safety.) In an e-mail message, I asked *Post* reporter Justin Gillis why the misleading headline? He told me that when a colleague of his pressed the FDA for an official vote count "they insisted, under challenge," that their numbers were accurate. "Of course, they arguably have a conflict of interest," noted Gillis. "At a minimum, we screwed up by not laying out that those numbers were an FDA staff interpretation."

The *Post* later printed the following clarification: "A November 5 Business article mischaracterized the actions of a Food and Drug Administration advisory committee studying animal cloning as an agricultural tool. The reported sentiment of the committee—that an eight to two majority supported the FDA's tentative conclusion that risks of eating cloned animals were minimal while members split five to five on whether cloning could pose excessive risks to animals—was based on informal polls by the chairman, not on formal votes."

To date there has been no independent, nonindustry sponsored study of the risks of cloned animal meat and milk, which may in fact already be present in our food supply.

* * *

In Rosalie's little red, organic barn, you find thirty Holstein cows listening to 1970s music from a portable radio. "See how their hair has grown long with the cold weather," she says, picking gently at one. Even though spring had arrived it was still chilly outside and they were confined to the indoors. "You should see them when they're back in the sun and eating grass," she says. "Their coats become really beautiful and shiny again. They'll be so happy."

Holsteins, she tells me, feel quite secure when they're all together, and don't have much of a flight instinct. Their famous curiosity is obvious as they make concerted efforts to twist their bodies toward a visiting stranger, who can't help feeling the effects of thirty pairs of gentle, brown eyes watching her every move. When you move closer, they lick all parts of you: skin, clothes, and hair, with sloppy, dripping tongues.

In the old days, milking by hand meant carrying buckets of milk one by one to a vat and pouring them in, along with flies and debris. With modern, sanitary vacuum systems, a slick contraption with four rubber cups is attached to the cow's teats directly and once the suction is turned on, milk is channeled upward through shiny steel pipes mounted above the stalls. Today it goes from the cow to a large tank in the adjoining milk house without ever touching the air.

After she attaches cups to a young cow named "Misty," the cow blinks, slowly, and becomes very still, her soft brown eyes glazing over with a peaceful expression. Misty has a tipped uterus, says Rosalie, which makes her hard to breed. Her first calf, standing with three other babies in the opposite corner of the barn, was born just a month ago. The milk Misty is giving today will be for them, she says, dragging buckets of fresh, warm liquid to that side of the room. The calves slurp hungrily from the bucket, and when it is gone, reach for each other's mouths and ears, pulling and sucking from wherever they can, splashes of milk still dripping from their lips.

Valentine, who is four and has given birth three times, slurps a mouthful of water and pours it from her own lips over Misty's head while licking and cleaning her face. "They take care of each other," offers Rosalie when I squeal in delight at the tender display of affection. "You should see them out in the pasture," she adds. "They lay out in groups and lean on each other. They're a herd. Very communal."

Traditional farmers push more grain, explains Rosalie, when I ask about the difference between organic and conventional farming. "That causes stress and mastitis in the udders, which is like an ulcer. It's awful. Like a nasty cottage cheese." In order to treat such problems, cows become accustomed to penicillin and needles. Organic farmers, in contrast, use mostly grass and organic hay, which is better for the land and gives cows more protein. As for shooting cows up with the artificial hormone rGBH to increase their production, Rosalie says this: "As a woman, imagine what it would feel like to add another three or four pounds of breast milk to what you would naturally produce. The animal's going to be stressed, and she's not going to live as long."

"All those big farms care about is the money," adds Clifford, who has been sweeping manure. Erionah, who spends her days with her grandparents while her mother is at work, darts in and out of the stalk as they work.

Rosalie Williams, whose family owns more than two hundred acres of land, is what they call "land rich and cash poor." Even an organic dairy, with its substantially higher rate of return, is not a particularly lucrative business for a small farmer. The average cow on Rosalie's farm nets less than $200 a year. She keeps a bull for breeding (as troublesome as they can be, she still prefers them to artificial insemination), a few pigs, and several dozen chickens that offer a couple dozen eggs a day, but for all the mess and trouble, small-time dairy farming is anything but a high-profit venture.

Next door to the red barn that houses Rosalie's cows and chickens and pigs lives her aunt, eighty-three-year-old Leona Snide. This part of town is even more isolated than the main road where Rosalie and Clifford live. Looking out onto the nearby mountain ranges from a lookout point on Peaked Hill Road, one can see land for miles around that now belongs to Rosalie alone. There are dozens of towering pine trees, planted by Leona when she was a young woman. The air here is still and cool. A family of deer passes us casually without a second glance.

Later that afternoon, I found Leona resting in an easy chair inside of her trailer home, which is filled with plastic knick-knacks and stuffed animals and toys for Erionah. Framed pictures cover every wall and table surface. When Rosalie was fifteen, Leona officially adopted her and she remains today, "the only mother I've ever known," says Rosalie.

After eight of her ten brothers and sisters moved away to start their own families, Leona, who never married, stayed on the farm, which she worked with the help of two remaining brothers: Raymond, who lived nearby with his wife and children, and Robert, who was mentally handicapped and stayed at home with Leona. Raymond was killed in a car accident in 1979 and in 1989 Robert died in a house fire. That was when Leona gave up tending cows and moved into a trailer home behind the barn and the ruins of her burnt house.

Towns folk never cared for her family, says Leona, and she never cared for them. In her younger days, she rode her horse along the dirt road, shunning cars. Everything her family needed was right there on the farm: eggs, vegetables, milk, meat, fruit, and juice. The only thing they bought from the store was paper towels.

To this day, Leona has never spoken about the mystery of Rosalie's race.

"My parents divorced when I was six months old," says Rosalie, "I guess because my father didn't believe I was his child." On weekends, when her father came to the farm to visit, Rosalie remembers him and her paternal grandfather having "awful fights" in which her name was mentioned often. Of her childhood memories, one that stands out is being onstage at age seven, preparing to sing in the school chorus when suddenly, a parent yanked her child right off the stage, away from Rosalie's side. She remembers her grandfather speaking with the parent later that evening outside. Ever since then, she says, people in town have always made a point to refer to her as "Vance Snides's granddaughter."

She also remembers having a babysitter, a black woman who lived in St. Albans. Something was odd about the arrangement, she says, citing a child's memory of blurred, overheard conversations. "I think her husband was my father." When her biological mother was dying of colon cancer in Florida, Rosalie got on a train to ask her again, for the final time, about her heritage. Her response was heartbreaking. "Your father's your father," she said, "I already told you that."

Shortly after, when the man Rosalie knew as her father also died of cancer, Rosalie was crushed by the fact that her own name was conspicuously missing from his obituary in a local newspaper because the woman he had lived with for twenty-seven years left it off. "Hell broke loose," recalls Rosalie, when her aunt Leona called the paper and demanded a correction.

Two years later, another family scandal broke out when the *Burlington Free Press* documented an ongoing "family feud" between Rosalie, her uncle Raymond, and his son, Anthony. In small claims court, Rosalie alleged that Tony had shot at her, and that her cows had been poisoned, spooked, and injured by fireworks that caused them to run through a barbed-wire fence. Perhaps even more upsetting than the attacks was her uncle Raymond's testimony before the judge. Yes, his brother's name was on Rosalie's birth certificate, he acknowledged, but she was in fact a "Negro" with a black father. "As far as I'm concerned," he said, "she was not part of our family" and did not deserve to inherit family land. "No Negro," he added, "should own land." (The judge ruled that the Snides were indeed responsible for the misdeeds and ordered them to pay $3,500 in damages.)

When I ask Leona, who also now has cancer, why she thinks the town dislikes her niece so, there is an excruciatingly long pause as she considers the question. I sense that she's trying to decide whether or not to set the words free, finally, out into the open air. But she hesitates, finally shrugging her shoulders. "Jealous," she says, the quiet air falling between us once again.

* * *

One of the first things you notice upon entering the home of Rosalie and Clifford Williams are the dozens of cardboard boxes and plastic crates stacked high along every available wall and in every inch of space throughout the kitchen and dining room, den, and an outside storage room. Food is everywhere. In addition to a standard refrigerator there is a commercial-sized Pepsi freezer case crammed into the dining area and stuffed full with great plastic tubs of cream cheese and gourmet vegetable dips. Clifford, a licensed hunter, has contributed three large deer heads to the décor, on living-room walls. A large wild turkey, also shot by Clifford, sits on a shelf by the front door, waiting to be deep-fried.

"We're big on food around here," says Rosalie, popping the trunk of her car to reveal still more goodies. "Look," she says, waving at stacks of commercial baked goods. There are three-layer frosted chocolate cakes, lemon muffins, cherry and apple pies, blueberry turnovers, apple strudels, sesame and onion bagels, and loaves and loaves of multigrain organic bread.

The food is for a massive monthly giveaway that she calls "Rosalie's Backseat Market," for low-income families and senior citizens. She's not really set up for such a large operation here, she says, gesturing toward her surroundings. Each year she gives away over 252,000 pounds of food collected from the USDA and private donations. She would like to have a building for storage. The giveaway takes place in an open field three miles down the road from Leona's trailer, on land recently purchased by Rosalie. Thirty minutes before distribution is scheduled to begin, dozens of cars have already snaked into a line behind the truck where volunteers pack and unload bags. Later, Rosalie's daughter Terah and Clifford work for hours, loading food into car trunks and backseats. On this day alone, 181 families will each receive Hannaford baked goods, ten tubs of cream cheese, concentrated apple and cranberry juice, six cans of cooked yams and corn, a whopping eight pounds of oatmeal, four pounds of spaghetti, whole figs, and lunchbox-sized puddings.

The families I had imagined in my mind when Rosalie first told me about the giveaway were a grateful, smiling bunch who embraced her family warmly as they exchanged small-town talk about local goings-on. But that didn't happen here. Something was amiss. Instead, the townspeople pulling up in cars struck me as oddly subdued, their gratitude offered through pursed lips. Many had dry, cracked skin and wore heavily stained work clothes; some wore cynical expressions as they blew cigarette smoke, one arm hanging from the windows of dirty pickup trucks. Other than small children, almost no one got out of their cars to say hello, offer a handshake, a hug, or a word of affection. Or maybe I was reading too much into it;

it was hard to be sure. Rosalie was noncommittal when I asked if she thought the town behaved coldly at the giveaway. Later she admitted that yes, some were probably racist, but she just tried to ignore them. One thing was sure: Rosalie and her family, with their smooth, healthy skin and unstained clothes, stood out from the crowd.

In July of 2004, during an ice cream fund-raiser for her organization, Rosalie was shut down by a Bakersfield zoning administrator who claimed that she needed a restaurant license from the town clerk to operate food carts. She replied that she was already licensed with the Secretary of State as a vendor and was regularly inspected by the Vermont Department of Health. If she needed a restaurant license, argued Rosalie, who later showed up at the administrator's home to clarify the matter, then so too did the local fire department, the historical society, the church, the Boy Scouts, and even kids selling lemonade off food carts, all of whom held similar fundraisers. She believes that her organization is being "discriminated against and harassed." She claims she does not know why exactly. But I think she does.

* * *

Clifford Williams's parents moved to Bakersfield from Connecticut when he was ten. Oddly, he too believes that, like

Rosalie, he was never told who his real father was. He shows me photographs of his cousin Steven, who is clearly brown-skinned, as well as his half-brother, Clarence, who is even darker. Clifford himself has identical coloring to Rosalie. With their matching buzz haircuts, they could be siblings. "There were black men, field hands working the tobacco farms near where I grew up," says Clifford. "And I would bet my life's salary that my father and Steven's father were the same man. My mother and aunt," he adds, "were always together. *Always* together."

He admits that over the years both he and Rosalie have had to deal with painful personal questions about family secrets and their own identities. Perhaps this is part of the reason they were drawn to one another—the only two nonwhite people in the entire town. Clifford and I just "kind of trimmed ourselves from our own family tree," says Rosalie. At this, tears come to her eyes and she pauses. Clifford's mother never remembered any of her grandchildren's birthdays, she says. "Our kids didn't really get to have grandparents on either side. Leona was the only one who really cared about them."

When a journalist enters your life and writes about you, whether or not the story that is told receives a wide audience or a small one, you are inevitably changed. "After you left," Rosalie tells me later by phone, "Clifford and I sat down and talked for two hours about being biracial." Conversations we'd had while I was there really "stirred things up" for both of them, she said. After I left, Clifford, who normally doesn't talk about this to anyone, even called his cousin Steven, to talk some more.

"I feel good," says Rosalie, "like I can really be myself for the first time." In fact, she even "went around town," proudly telling people that "a *black woman's magazine writer* came and spent *three* days with me." But I can't help wondering whether or not visiting her and raising these questions is really something she can handle. When the book is published, I offer, you'll still have to live here. What will happen if the people in Bakersfield read it?

"*And?*" she says bitterly. "I'm never gonna get support from my town. Clifford has tried to show me how people are, but I was always so protected. I never had to defend myself." Even their children were teased in school and called "half-breeds" growing up. And when Clifford's brother Clarence came to town, a former boyfriend of Terah's was troubled. "If we have children together," he asked, "will they have little Afros?" She ended the relationship immediately, says Rosalie. "Never even gave him a second chance."

And yet, Rosalie seems to exercise a kind of willful obliviousness about the towns' long-standing snubs. Her multipurpose building will go right here in the open field, she announces, after the food giveaway. Once that's in place, it will be easier to organize both the food and her summer camp for at-risk youth.

But sometimes kids say they can't come to camp because their parents "don't like dark people." Either way, she does this work for one reason and one reason alone: she does it for her son, U.S. Marine Lucas James Williams, who was killed in Kuwait in 1998 at the age of nineteen.

* * *

Vermont has over eight hundred thousand acres of wildlife habitat for hunting. There are black bears, moose, wild turkeys, white-tailed deer, geese, ducks, hares, squirrels, woodcocks, and ruffed grouse. There are also five thousand miles of snowmobile trails and sixty-six ski areas, the greatest concentration anywhere in the world. And unlike many of the latchkey kids in the area who now spend their hours zoned out in front of a television, Lucas saw freedom and possibility in nature: hunting, fishing, anything outdoors. In fact, his famous bonfires held on the rock ledges above the family barn were known throughout the area for attracting hundreds of youths.

"It bothered Lucas when kids didn't have money to do things," recalls Rosalie, saying that many still come to her looking for work. "I try to give them something, even if it's only $5.00 an hour to help with fencing or cleaning the barn."

Six months after Lucas's death, she purchased ten and a half acres of land (the open field that her family now calls "the property"), with a clear water creek for swimming, and founded the Lucas James Williams Youth Memorial Fund to provide exposure to the kind of life Lucas believed kids should have, "outdoors, away from the television."

Everything on the grounds is donated. There is sand and nets for volleyball courts; a small, aboveground wading pool; trampolines; horseshoe pits; trailers stuffed with industrial-size refrigerators and stoves; ice machines; a cold cart for ice-cream making and a hot cart for French fries; dartboards and a plastic "bounce castle" for small children; basketballs, soccer balls; a dunking booth; and even a miniature merry-go-round. On the edges of the field, there are several large wooden hut frames, built by Terah, for the famous Halloween Haunted Forest. In addition to the summer camp, which hosts nearly a hundred kids a year, there is an annual Fishing Derby held at a nearby one-acre trout pond stocked by the state under a program called Kids Brooks. To qualify for funds, Clifford became certified to teach a workshop in how to cast a line, bait a hook, and clean a fish, along with information about ecology. He also teaches hunter safety and bow-hunting. Prizes, donated by Pepsi, include mountain bikes for every age category.

There is a large organic vegetable garden on the property,

where senior citizens, children, and teenagers work side-by-side, learning about soil conservation and planting string beans, tomatoes, carrots, corn, cabbage, and broccoli. With food from the harvest and additional funding from the University of Vermont Cooperative Extension Service, Rosalie hosts a youth cooking class. Camp attendees also learn a healthy respect for the land through tree-planting, building wildlife habitats for birds and game, and designing deer yards and clearing areas for moose.

In a trade magazine published by *Organic Valley*, Rosalie is featured among a collage of children, who run toward the camera in shorts, T-shirts, towels, and bathing suits. In the winter, she organizes snowboarding and bobsledding parties. One day, she hopes to put in hiking trails on her family land high up in the mountains. And most of all, Rosalie hopes to erect a building on the property, where kids can have a gym and roller-skating rink and won't have to run home every time it rains. She is afraid that her dream won't materialize because of the town's narrow-mindedness. She uses the word "scary" often to describe the sudden growth of Lucas's Memorial Fund, which has received multiple grants and support from the Vermont Department of Alcohol and Substance Abuse Prevention Program, the Department of Health, the Department of Education, and the Champlain Valley Area on Aging, among others.

She knows it's time to grow Lucas's Memorial Fund. "I've been suffocating it," she says, "because of my fear."

* * *

Lucas loved pyrotechnics and "blowing up things," says Clifford, when asked why his son joined the military. "You'd be around the farm and you'd hear this big explosion. And it would be Lucas blowing up woodchuck holes." When recruiters arrived at his high school, the kid who was already six feet four was a sure thing. He was handsome and had a lot of girlfriends, says his sister Terah, when I ask if there was anyone special in his life. "He'd be sitting on the couch with one, talking on the phone to another. And then, when this one left out the back door, another one came in the front."

Sarah Jo Willey, Miss Vermont for 2002, remembers Lucas as being "full of life, fun-loving. He was tall and thin with the most amazing blue eyes. And a silly little grin on his face. In high school, he dyed his hair blue," she recalls, "so for a while he had this big curly mop of blue hair." And he had a "totally contagious, mischievous laugh. He was a quiet leader," she adds, "the guy who always had the plan."

When they were young, and he was her boyfriend, so to speak, in seventh grade, Lucas gave Sarah a Valentine's Day present of a box of chocolates and a teddy bear with a battery-operated heartbeat. Later, even though they went to different high schools, they remained close and she thought of him "like a brother." He was certainly a charmer, she says. "He was fun, and he knew how to treat people well." The last time Sarah saw Lucas he had come home on military leave and stopped by to see her family. "He was still Lucas," she says, "but he had matured. He was happy, doing something he really enjoyed. He gave me a big hug and I took a picture of him that I still have in a frame on my dresser."

With Lucas as the toe missile operator, the top half of his body exposed as he manned his unit's weaponry, his team was assigned to patrol the Iraqi-Kuwait border. At a special military hearing held in Japan, eleven Marines testified that the Humvee he rode in "flipped, and crushed him twice. I've had I don't know how many four-star generals tell me stories about how he died," says Rosalie. "None of them make any sense."

"It was a cupcake testimony they were giving," says Clifford, his face clouding with anger. "I mean, you could see the witness reading from a paper." It was a well-scripted show, they say. A cover-up. What really happened, believe Clifford and Rosalie, is that the young boys in Lucas's unit were "dusting," a high-stakes game where three Hummers take off at speeds of sixty-five miles per hour (the military limit is twenty-five miles per hour) racing and kicking up sand to blind the other drivers.

Lucas had called home just a few hours before his death on December 22, 1998. "I got my anthrax shot," he told his mother, adding that he was "good to go." "And he said good-bye," she recalls. "We never say good-bye. We always say, 'See you later.'" In the war in Iraq, Vermont residents currently suffer the highest national casualty rates, with that state's enlistees dying at three times the average rates of other states.

* * *

On February 13, 2002, Rosalie suffered a fall that left her paralyzed for eleven days. She likes to tell the story, though, of how she was mysteriously saved. We are standing on the second floor of the barn, in the hay mow, looking down through a square opening in the ceiling, a kind of trapdoor that is used to toss bales of hay down to the cows below. Rosalie is showing me how her foot slipped in this very spot, and she fell through the opening, catching herself at the last minute by reaching for the trapdoor. She remembers holding on with three fingers.

"I felt the vertebrae in my neck clicking," she says, "and I knew I wasn't going to survive hanging like that." And that's when things got strange. "I could see the back of my head suspended and my body ten feet from the floor as if I were watching the scene from somewhere else." She maintains that something or someone then grabbed her shin or her ankle and turned her upside down. "You know how you watch the room spinning?" she asks, trying to describe the blur of images. "I saw everything spin by, and then I was hanging by my feet."

She was later found seated in an upright "L" position with her legs stretched out in front of her, and her back propped against the steel bulk tank in the milk house. "There is no way I could have dragged myself into that room in the condition I was in," she says. And furthermore, "My clothes were clean. I would have had to climb through the cows to get where I was. How did I get to the milk house without getting dirty?"

Although her son had been dead for four years, Rosalie says that she heard his voice over and over again, calling out, and trying to get her attention as she sat paralyzed in the milk house. "You know how kids joke around? Well, it was like a child trying to annoy you. He kept saying, 'Mom. Mom. *Mom.* What's the number for 911?' My tongue was swollen. The only thing I could move was my eyes. And I could hear a woman's voice saying, 'If you'd like to make a call, please hang up and dial again.' And Lucas just kept asking me, *'Mom. What's the number for 911?'* So I finally said it: 'Nine-one-one.' And then the operator came on."

The strange part is that the barn's phone is mounted on the wall six feet above the ground. Rosalie was found paralyzed from the neck down. "We've never believed in spirits," she says, "but I've changed my mind since the accident. There's just no way I could have done what I did alone."

Today, she believes that there is a larger force at work, guiding everything she does with the Lucas James Williams Youth Memorial Fund. "I get feelings," she says. "Like once I was sitting on the couch, wondering where I could take the kids and I thought of a food cart idea and a bonfire. Just then, the phone rang and it was a friend in New York. I hadn't spoken to him in years. And he said, 'It was the funniest thing. I was on my lunch hour and thought I should call you. My ex-wife's got a food cart for sale.'" She ended up donating it to Rosalie and the kids for free.

"I've dialed numbers of people I didn't even know I was calling," she continues, "and there's always someone on the other line who picks up the phone and can help us with something." Like when she needed a part for an obsolete barbecue grill for the summer camp. "Sunbeam doesn't even make this part anymore," she says, "but I got this woman on the phone and it turns out that her son was leaving for Iraq and we started talking. She said, 'I'll go to the warehouse myself to look for the part.'"

Once, she says, she was sitting in the barn as the cows were milking, "just bawling my head off." Then suddenly, a cool dampness came over her. "I stood up and there was a person standing there, fifty feet away, wearing a blue flannel shirt and corduroy jeans." At this, she points to a framed photograph in the living room: an image of Lucas standing on a mountain top. He is wearing a blue flannel shirt and corduroy jeans. She didn't exactly hear the words with her ears, she says, but it's as though they were inside of her, "in my gut." It was a phrase she had often repeated to her kids, drumming it into their heads over and over again.

"You never fail, until you quit trying."

"I'm not afraid anymore," she says.

7.

Sarah White celebrating in happier days.

WORKER

Indianola, Mississippi

O f all the women in this book I have spent the most time with Sarah White. For many reasons her story is the one closest to my heart. When I began this project and wasn't quite sure what I was looking for, or what form my reporting would take, I was led to Indianola by a series of unplanned events and seemingly random guidance. Journalists are not supposed to become sentimentally attached to their subjects, but Sarah has changed me. She has moved me to a place beyond the person I was before.

I remember vividly my first visit to Indianola, Mississippi. It was 1996. In the decade since, I have returned to the South dozens of times, but back then it was all new to me. I remember driving down backwoods roads and thinking about movies like *Mississippi Burning* and what "they" might do to trouble-making journalists like me. I remember being dazzled by the six-foot high sunflowers growing in ordinary yards behind ordinary houses. And I remember sitting with five women around a conference table in the spare office of Local 1529 of the United Food and Commercial Workers Union in downtown Indianola. It was there, in an old brick building, that the women did their strategizing: planning union campaigns, and marking color-coded charts with the names of supporters, bags of fast-food splayed out before them. Their work involved setting up in dusty hotels sometimes for months at a time. Their mission was to convince rural workers to stand together for health benefits, living wages, paid holidays, and job security. Most importantly, the task of the union was to bring dignity to the lives of poor Southern women and men.

Indianola is in the heart of the Delta, a region where thousands of homes still do not have adequate plumbing and where a dozen counties have poverty rates above 30 percent. The few jobs that remain for low-skilled workers tend to be in factories, especially ones that process catfish. Before my first visit there, I had never heard of Sarah Claree White. Never read her name in any newspaper. I did not know that in 1990, at age thirty-one, she had helped to lead the largest strike of black workers ever to take place in the state of Mississippi.

Of course, Mississippi had a long history of black workers organizing. In 1866, poor washerwomen published a statement that read in part, "Whereas, under the influence of the present high prices of all the necessaries of life, and the attendant high rates of rent, while our wages remain very much reduced, we, the washerwomen of the city of Jackson, State of Mississippi, thinking it impossible to live uprightly and honestly in laboring for the present daily and monthly recompense, and hoping to meet with the support of all good citizens, join in adopting unanimously the following resolution . . . we join in charging a uniform rate for our labor . . . and any one belonging to the class of washerwomen, violating this, shall be liable to a fine regulated by the class."

According to the 1991 documentary *This Far by Faith*, the Delta Pride strike of nearly one thousand mostly black, female workers was "one of the most significant labor and civil rights victories of the decade."

So why hadn't I heard about it? Why hadn't I known that black women of the 1990s were leading movements as grand as anything the 1960s ever saw? Why was Sarah's battle any less newsworthy than the often-televised marches led by Dr. Martin Luther King? Why was there no media coverage or public awareness of ongoing civil rights struggles in the

South? I first went to Mississippi not knowing anything about Sarah White or Delta Pride. I went because my heart said "go." I trusted it to tell me why.

* * *

Lunch hour at Delta Pride takes place indoors, on wooden picnic benches, where workers eat their food still wearing blood-splattered work jackets and blue hairnets. There is no escape from the stench of fish. A few women carry fast food from Burger King. Most unpack plastic containers from home filled with beef, sweet potatoes, and chicken. No one eats catfish. They know too much about it. After lunch, the women play cards or rest their heads on the tables. As Reverend Jesse Jackson, Sr. once described them to me, "These are women who work all day and still live below the poverty line. Some eat lunch standing up, a chicken sandwich in one hand, cigarette in the other."

When Delta Pride came to Indianola in 1981, Sarah White was twenty-two and a new mother to her first child, Antoine. Her son's father was a farm worker in his forties who ran a small country juke joint and left the parenting to Sarah. She worked at the nearby Con Agra catfish plant at first, but found it difficult to keep up with the night shift (the only hours that company had available), and care for her son, too. So, in 1983, she took a job at Delta Pride where she beheaded, gutted, and skinned catfish for up to thirteen hours a day. For this, work she earned $3.40 an hour, five cents more than minimum wage. The company's arrival felt like a new beginning in a town where opportunities were hard to come by. It was a chance for single women to get off the welfare lines, as Sarah once put it, and to make a better life for themselves and their children.

But the reality was that conditions at Delta Pride were no different from those of hundreds of poultry, catfish, tobacco, and steel plants all across the South. Workers were routinely denied medical treatment for carpal tunnel syndrome (a nerve injury caused by repetitive hand movement), burns from scalding hot water, and eye injuries from splashing bleach and ammonia water. No sick days were allowed; if you or your child became ill and you stayed home, you risked being fired. In response to injury complaints, company nurses distributed aspirin and sent employees back to their stations to continue working. Other than Christmas Day, there were no holidays and hands were never allowed to slow or rest. There was barely time to wipe the fish blood off your face.

About 90 percent of Delta's workforce was black and female. In the 1980s, the company was owned by a farming collective of 178 white men. (It is currently down to about 160.) Before the union, white male supervisors would routinely harass workers, sexually and verbally. "They would come up behind you and feel on you," recalls Sarah. "They'd ask where you live, and say that if they could come by and see you, they'd put you on an easier job." According to several workers I spoke with during my visits, supervisors were "right behind you all the time pressuring you to go faster. 'Why'd you even leave home today?' they would say. 'All you're good for is making babies.'"

In video footage taken by a UFCW documentary film-maker, a white, female Delta supervisor explains on-camera that the majority of workers at the plant are illiterate and unskilled and, therefore, not deserving of higher raises. Sarah's comeback is classic: "I may not have my degree in cuttin' heads," she offers. "But if you put me through twenty years of hard work I should be paid for that work. You and me go in the store and pay the same amount of money for a loaf of bread."

As Mississippi poet and journalist Charlie Braxton explained, "Working at these factories is like being on a plantation." In fact, he added, "The people who run the catfish farms are related to the same people who ran the plantations. They're on the same family land." Historian Clyde Woods agrees. As he writes in his book *Development Arrested: Race, Power, and the Blues in the Mississippi Delta*, plantation families didn't just disappear after slavery. "They simply expanded their monopolies over agriculture, banking, land, and water." In recent years, the Centennial Farms program, established by the Mississippi Department of Agriculture and Commerce, has documented at least 215 farming families who have "owned, produced crops, and passed on to new generations the same acres in the same places" for at least a century. "Often," states the program's Web site, "the farm sizes have grown extensively under the family ownership umbrellas."

"Inside these catfish and poultry plants," says Braxton, "you walk in boots because your feet are covered in entrails and blood. It's the worst kind of work you could possibly do." Braxton, who has written for hip-hop magazines such as *Vibe* and *The Source*, went on to tell me about a young man who lasted exactly eight hours at the B.C. Rogers poultry plant in McComb, Mississippi, where mostly female workers skinned chickens, hung them, and ripped off the breasts at an astonishing rate of thirty-two birds per minute. The kid couldn't handle it. "This guy came out and his hands were all bloody and raw," recalls Braxton, "and he said, 'Man, I can't do this.' He ended up selling crack. That life was more appealing to him."

By far the most perverse evidence of "plantation mentality" at Delta was the company's bathroom policy, whereby workers had to ask for permission, like children, to relieve themselves. Often, they were refused. Tales of women and men urinating on the processing line (or wearing diapers as a precaution) were common. And when permission was granted, supervisors followed close behind with a timer. Outside breaks, workers were allowed five minutes per week for what they called bathroom "privileges." At Delta, the stall doors had even been removed to discourage "dawdling."

Charlie Braxton notes that many young black men in the South have refused to accept these conditions. "Their anger is coming out in hip-hop," he said, "and they aren't going into these plants. Young people are saying they'd rather go to jail, or join the army and risk getting killed."

When I ask Sarah where black men are in the struggle, her answer comes fast and hard. "In jail. On drugs. Or pursuing careers and don't care about us."

In 1985, Sarah's son was four, and she didn't see the army or selling drugs as options. What was an option was signing the union card her coworker, Mary Young, had received in the mail. It was a bold move that meant risking her job and even her safety. Although freedom of association is guaranteed by the U.S. Constitution, a 1999 survey of four hundred organizing campaigns by Cornell University and the National Labor Relations Board found that 25 percent of employees attempting to organize were illegally fired by their employers. Incidents of intimidation and harassment are believed to be much higher.

But Sarah and Mary were fed up. "It just seemed like they

had control of our minds," recalls Sarah, "and nobody understood that we could break through to a better place." They spent that winter secretly making house calls, collecting signatures, and standing outside the local Wal-Mart in the cold, in an effort to persuade workers to band together. After two months of "driving around in Mary's old unheated jalopy," as Sarah puts it, they had successfully built an organizing committee of fifty workers: enough to bring the union in for a vote. As Jackson-based UFCW Representative Sylvester Fields tells me, "The worst thing owners can have in a plant is some *mad black women.*"

"Ya'll know anything about a union coming here?" asked their supervisors.

"No, ma'am."

"Because you'll be fired you know, if you're involved."

"Yes, ma'am."

Their victory came during the Christmas season of 1986. The UFCW was voted in at Delta and Sarah was overjoyed. "We got three-year contracts saying we had job security," she recalled. "And we got right to use the bathroom six times a week, five minutes each time." In spite of all this, harassment just got worse. "We were good to you before," threatened management. "We gave you catfish for the holidays, but that's over now."

At the same time, hazardous work conditions remained unchanged. Sarah herself suffered second- and third-degree burns when scalding hot water crept through her work boots. And in 1989, Delta was fined $32,800 by the United States Occupational Safety and Health Administration (OSHA) for failing to prevent and treat carpal tunnel syndrome among workers. During contract negotiations and in response to a list of grievances presented by unionized workers in 1990, management once again threatened to take away bathroom rights.

It was the final humiliation: a psychological blow that was felt across generations. This time workers did what had once been unimaginable. They walked.

"It wasn't pretty," says Sarah. There were gunshots fired at night near the picket lines, intimidation tactics, and hostile "cursing back and forth" on both sides during the standoff. As the battle escalated, she and several coworkers were invited to Washington, D.C., to testify before members of the Congressional Black Caucus. It was a pivotal decision. There, the stories of the women at Delta garnered publicity and support for a nationwide consumer boycott spearheaded by Reverend Jesse Jackson. Soon major grocers in several cities such as St. Louis, Chicago, Atlanta, and Detroit were refusing to stock Delta Pride fish.

It is always baffling to me that so many young people today turn their noses up at "old-fashioned" strategies of strikes and boycotts. Hitting corporate power where it hurts, their bottom line, has always been effective. In the case of Delta, the combined effects of boycotts and striking workers, plus international disdain for their policies, brought the company to its knees after just three months. In December of 1990, Local 1529 received a contract guaranteeing workers seven paid holidays a year, time and a half after eight hours of work, a pension plan, the right to a harassment-free work environment, medical treatment for work-related injuries, and the right to use bathrooms *as needed*.

* * *

Yet fifteen years after this staggering victory, Sarah's personal and professional struggles are far from over. Once the union arrived, she was made a union mediator and organizer, which means that she is both inside the UFCW offices, the plant, and the homes of workers, where she documents problems and handles conflict resolution. In the past decade, Delta management has done extensive renovations to create a safer work environment, although Mississippi was still one of eight states in 2003 that did not monitor or record workplace injuries. But there are new problems: the company's increased mechanization (financed with nearly $10 million in taxpayer loans through the USDA) means that fewer workers are needed. And even today, some with twenty years of seniority still make as little as $7.00 an hour.

What's more, many of Sarah's greatest challenges come from within the union itself, which she believes is guilty of unfair compensation structures. Her struggles are internal too, tied to her own sense of self-worth and self-love.

"My mom was a single parent with ten children," she says, when asked about her childhood growing up in Inverness, Mississippi. Sarah's father deserted his family "to go with another lady," as she puts it, after a car accident (he was driving) that left her mother in a coma and later, disabled after multiple knee and hip surgeries. "My mom worked in white women's homes cleaning and ironing," she says, and picking cotton, which Sarah also did as a child. "I don't regret my childhood but it was poor. We wore homemade clothes. My mother did the best she could."

Her maternal grandparents had good jobs in St. Louis, Missouri, where her grandmother cleaned houses for "rich white doctors" and her grandfather did mechanical work on railroads. They sent hand-me-down clothing, toys, and colorful books from the families they worked for. Good stuff, says Sarah. Thanks to her grandmother's employers, she and five siblings were the first children in the neighborhood to have one shiny red bicycle, which they all shared. But as a teenager, Sarah was painfully shy and ashamed of her rundown shoes and the simple dresses her mother sewed for her to wear to school. All the while, she saw her father working a good farm job nearby, with "a nice house, nice car, and kids that had nice clothes. I was kind of jealous that we had to go without," she admits. "It bothers me to this day. He hurt my mother and then he left her hurt."

"Mama would say, 'Get a better job. Don't end up like me,'" she recalls. So Sarah was grateful to receive a four-year scholarship to Mississippi Valley State University. She graduated with a Bachelor of Science degree in Elementary School Education at twenty-two, and worked as a substitute teacher while studying for her teacher's certification. "I took that test twice," she says. "I passed my areas, but I never could pass the general stuff, like arts. Failed by eight points."

It didn't have to be that way.

In 2001, when Sarah was forty-three, the State of Mississippi agreed to spend $500 million (money that is still held up in appeal) to improve the state's historically black colleges —Jackson State, Alcorn State, and Mississippi Valley State—which were found by federal courts to be "vastly inferior to the colleges that whites attended." The victory came about as a result of a civil rights case initiated in 1975 by a black sharecropper named Jake Ayers on behalf of his son. It is possible that the $500 million might have added up to a different future for Sarah, had the case not dragged on for two and a half decades. But when I ask why she didn't keep trying to pass the test for her teaching credential Sarah's answer pulls at my heart. "I guess I just didn't have the smarts," she says. "I lost interest after a while."

After a while, she took a much-needed job at Delta Pride, where she would remain over two decades later.

Often, when I would call or visit, I found Sarah feeling defeated and depressed. One summer evening just after 11 P.M., we sat across from one another at her dining-room table. Outside, her Ford Taurus was parked alongside a low wall of thick weeds separating her home from the railroad tracks. The humidity was heavy and the crickets deafening. Cherry Coke in one hand and plastic flyswatter in the other, Sarah took her time answering my questions as she paused for long, contemplative drags from a Benson and Hedges cigarette while formulating her thoughts. Occasionally she cracked a smile, flashing a shiny gold front tooth, but on this particular night, she was mostly gloomy. Her ongoing battle was for living wages, but even as a union representative, she said, she often went for years at a time without a raise.

"I get stressed out," she admitted, "and sometimes right there in the office, I gotta go in the back room and cry it out. I'm out here in these plants all day trying to turn this thing 'round the best I can. From Tunica down to Yazoo, catfish houses . . . I'm trying to take care of people: issues, problems, terminations, all kind of stuff."

Once, in the mid-1990s, I had the opportunity to watch

Sarah at work as a union liaison, mediating complaints between workers and management. It was a learning experience to be sure. We traveled to the Delta plant in Belzoni to discuss the suspension of a worker named Milton. Sitting on wooden chairs in a plain office, we faced a white, female supervisor with dirty blond hair, named Lisa. Milton, who joined us still wearing his white overcoat and hairnet, had been suspended for refusing to work a double shift, even though he hadn't been given any advance notice. Prior to this suspension, he had been fired and quickly rehired—a common company practice that cuts costs by bringing workers back on at minimum wage.

The tension in the room was thick. Lisa, the supervisor, claimed that she didn't have any grievance forms filed by Milton, which, according to one union representative, he had "sat down under a tree and wrote two pages on." Opening and closing wooden drawers in a show of searching for the forms, Lisa sighed and tossed a pile of yellow sheets across the desk toward Sarah, adding, "These here is all I got."

For a moment, no one spoke.

The only sound in the room was the click-click of a ball-point pen in Lisa's hand.

Turning her attention to a nearby window, Sarah fixed her gaze somewhere outside as she paused to collect her thoughts. Then, she turned and addressed Milton alone, in evenly measured tones. "We got a grievance procedure here at Delta. That means that you say what you need to say. As far as if somebody not treating you with respect, or harassing you, or not treating you like a man, you have a voice through this union. So now, Milton. You got the floor."

Milton was a shy, small-framed, brown-skinned man. "Well," he began. "I basically feel like I'm doing the job of two men. I start at 9 A.M. and I stays sometime until 11 at night. There's a man who supposed to be helping me," he continued, "they call him the ice man . . . but he don't wear no gloves or coat. He just walk around."

Sarah took it all in and continued, speaking only to Milton.

"As far as with Lisa, she supposed to have a open-door policy where you can come and file your grievance. But if she don't hear you, or won't hear you, you can come to us. You know, Milton," she added, "you doing your job, you got a family to feed, Lisa doing her job, she got a family to feed . . . But you gotta be careful with that strain, working them hours. If you have a problem and need medical treatment . . . you know . . ." Here she paused: "They might need to think about if things need to be redone in that area. *Delta*." It was plantation diplomacy in its most subtle form. Milton would never be promoted to supervisor or raise his standard of living by working at Delta, but with Sarah there, he might at least hang onto his paycheck and a shred of dignity.

* * *

In the summer of 2005, fifteen years after the union came to Delta Pride, I found that Sarah's depression had worsened and the years of stress had begun to wear on her. She wore no makeup this time, and there were dark circles under her eyes. She had also gained weight and two near-empty bottles of hypertension medication sat in a basket on her office desk. Just three months earlier she had been hospitalized with congestive heart failure and high blood pressure. When I first met her, a trimmer more energetic Sarah had greeted me wearing a cute, leatherette vest and fashionable black sandals. This time, she wore a shapeless dress and a sweater, even though it was hot and humid outside.

Citing harassment, nit-picking, and disrespectful faxes and comments from a superior, Sarah had actually resigned her position with the union after her release from the hospital. She was tired, she said, of being forced to work on weekends and during her vacation time; tired of the stress and constant pressure to "work a miracle down here" as she put it. She had always admired Fannie Lou Hamer and related to her sadness. "People say that she never did recover from that beating they gave her. And she was a sad lady because no matter how much she struggled, things just didn't get better."

Whereas workers had won the right to time and a half pay

after eight hours of work in 1990, they were now back to regular pay for up to nine or ten hours of labor, as long as the company stayed within a forty-hour workweek. The union had lost ground. With the threat of foreign markets at every corner (Vietnamese catfish was apparently making a dent in Delta's revenue), the company held the promise of bankruptcy over negotiators' heads, and it sometimes seemed like they meant it. Delta, which had three plants and nearly a thousand workers when the union first came, now had only one plant and, with increased mechanization, the workforce was down to 460 employees.

But what surprised me most about Sarah during this visit is that she agreed to stay on at Delta—despite the pressures, her health, and a paltry pay raise from $26,000 to $28,000. In fact, she had actually been offered another job paying $36,000 by her friend Jaribu Hill, executive director of the Mississippi Worker's Center for Human Rights in Greenville. Her reasons for turning it down remain unclear, even to me. Over the years Sarah had spoken to me often of Jaribu, calling her someone she "admires to the fullest" and "a true friend." An active supporter of the Center, Sarah's image is featured prominently on the organization's Web site. Perhaps she believed that the union would do better than the $2,000 pay increase, or that the stressful harassment would improve. When I ask her why she turned

Jaribu down, she seems genuinely stumped herself, saying, "I don't know. I haven't figured that one out yet."

Years earlier she had been offered yet another union job with the potential to advance to $60,000 within just a few years. She turned that one down too because it meant frequent travel and she worried that there would be no one to take care of her grandchildren, now five and three, and largely in her care. Her unemployed daughter, Tangelia, still lives at home, and in March of 2005 (the same month that Sarah was hospitalized), she gave birth to her third child. Sarah is also raising her ex-boyfriend's nephew, now twelve, who has been in her care since he was a baby. The logical solution might be to tell Tangelia to get a job and take more responsibility for the care of her own children. Sarah knows this. Jaribu has been telling her for years: stop letting people take advantage of her.

We spent a lot of time during our last visit talking about Sarah's work and personal life. Union organizing ended her childhood shyness, she once said, but she continues to find it difficult to ask for what she deserves. Instead of speaking clearly about what she will and will not accept, she has a habit of "carrying things around sometimes for months," holding the frustration inside. "Sometimes I take abuse and people will mistreat me and I won't say nothing," she says.

So why does she stay at Delta?

"The only reason I hang on here is because of love of a dream. But you can't work when it's pressure on you from all sides. You know," she admits, "the thought of me going to Jaribu and accepting that job, felt so much better." But I know that she will not leave Delta and the union. Not yet anyway.

Her doctor says she needs to cut back on the salt and cigarettes. She was up to two packs a day. "He told me I need to lose some weight, too, but I just don't *feel* like it. He say gotta cut down on fried foods but that's all we eat down here. I cook fried chicken or pork chops with rice. We don't eat greens or cabbage. Not that I don't like it. I just don't have time. And we get so used to fast food." I tell her I want her to live a long life and be healthy. I babble on about the importance of diet and exercise and although she agrees at first, eventually a shadow falls across her face and I can tell I'm getting on her nerves. Later, at dinner, she glances up at me before ordering grilled shrimp (even though she really wanted fried) and a salad, adding under her breath, "You killin' me, Kristal."

The Fannie Lou Hamer Sister Roundtable is a quarterly event organized by the Mississippi Workers' Center for Human Rights; a "gathering of black women workers, elected officials, social-justice advocates and others to address obstacles women face in struggling to improve conditions in their communities." Recently, Sarah attended the roundtable and, as a journaling exercise, wrote a letter that she wants me to hear.

Reaching for a black-and-white composition notebook, she says that the instruction was to take ten minutes to write to the person who inspired you.

"You wrote to Fannie Lou?" I ask.

"Yeah, you know me. I wrote to Fannie."

"I first heard of you years ago," she told her hero, "when I worked in this plantation-style plant where women had no voice . . . I became a member of the Mississippi Workers Center and part of the Fannie Lou Hamer Sister Roundtable to bring your message home. I want you to know," she continued in the letter, "that even though I did not know you, I feel your spirit so deeply and your work. I want you to know that your fire will be my fire."

The next morning, a strange synchronicity was at work when I received an e-mail about a fellowship program I had never heard of: the Alston-Bannerman Fellowship. The organization was offering $15,000 in funds to be used as a three-month sabbatical for "longtime activists of color." They could "recharge and reenergize" using their time to "travel, study, visit with other activists, read, relax, explore new interests . . . plan or just be still." Charles Bannerman, I learned, had worked for twenty years with the Mississippi Action for Community Education (MACE), which happened to have been founded by Fannie Lou Hamer herself. I printed the information and dropped it in the mail, knowing that there was little chance she would apply.

I sent it anyway.

For Sarah.

8.

Candace & Bruce Matthews

EXECUTIVE

New York, New York

The youngest of eighteen children, Candace Matthews was born in New Brighton, Pennsylvania, to a Methodist preacher father and a homemaker mother. Her parents were extremely traditional, she says. "My mother fixed my father's plate for every meal and sat it down in front of him. She cooked a hot breakfast every morning, dinner was ready by 4:30 P.M. and the family was in bed by 8:30." When I ask about her mother's character she says, "You know how they say babies and children can tell the soul of a person? She could hold a baby in her arms and it would just feel her and stop crying. She had what they call that ol' lady rock.'"

As a Methodist preacher, Candace says that her father's style was more "serene and articulate" than "fire and brimstone." In addition to ministering, he worked a second job at the Westinghouse Electric Company, and a third as the owner of his own painting company, which also employed his sons. "I got a tremendous work ethic from him," explains Candace. "I can still remember him rubbing his hands with turpentine and Lava soap at the end of the day. That soap was so hard, it was like pumice. But that's how he had to get the paint off, by rubbing that bar on his fingers. I remember that extremely vividly." Candace was just ten, the baby of the family, when her father died of a heart attack at the age of sixty-six.

It was 1969 and Candace's mother didn't know a thing about managing finances. "For a while we went on public assistance and I got free lunches in high school," she recalls. "Things you wouldn't have imagined." At a very young age "I had to learn how to write checks and balance the checkbook for my mother." She recalls how the family would have a big salad to go with dinner but only one bottle of dressing to be shared by everyone. Since her brothers dominated at the table, there was never enough. Because of that, "I grew up not liking salad," says Candace, who today keeps a dozen bottles of dressing in her cupboards at all times. Her childhood fears about poverty left an indelible mark on her psyche. "I'm not a spender," she says, "and I won't go into debt. If I can't afford it, I don't buy it."

Despite their poverty, sixteen of the family's children went on to college. Candace received her Bachelor of Science in metallurgical engineering and administrative management from Carnegie-Mellon University in Pittsburgh and later, a Master's in Business Administration from Stanford University in California. "My family was very big on education," she says. Her brother Larry, who is ten years her senior, was hired at IBM, where he stayed for twenty-five years. His position had a "tremendous influence" on young Candace. While her father gave her a role model for entrepreneurship and hard work, Larry proved that there was a place at the table for African Americans, inside of corporate America.

* * *

I had expected to see her assistant Nicole, after being buzzed through the security intercom at the glass-door entrance to her offices on Fifth Avenue and Forty-Seventh Street. Instead, Candace greeted me herself, offering a hug rather than a handshake and addressing me with wide, animated brown eyes. Wearing a simple gray pantsuit and low-heeled walking pumps with dark stockings, she moved through the halls quickly, binding her words into tight, fast-paced bundles that were delivered with the youthful tenor of an energetic college sophomore.

I had first met the high-powered executive at a midtown Manhattan conference for professional women of color, sponsored by *Working Mother* magazine, where I had worked as a guest editor. The conference hosted hundreds of vice presidents and senior managers from the highest echelons of corporate America. As the women roamed the Sheraton hotel ballrooms, I, a self-employed freelance writer, surprised myself with a strange mix of emotions. Much as I love my work (my words, my soul) I couldn't help feeling a tinge of envy for the nine-to-fivers. They had chosen to patiently carve out financial stability for themselves; to pick a job and stay there, despite the challenges. They were tenacious achievers with the strength of character to work on teams, even when their coaches and owners weren't up to snuff.

As president of SoftSheen-Carson, the world's leading provider of hair- and skin-care products for people of African descent, Candace had been a panelist at the banquet luncheon, looking decidedly glamorous with glossy lips, freshly pressed curls, and a stylish three-quarter length business jacket. She spoke with refreshing candor—about marrying for the first time at the age of forty, struggling with infertility, and constantly striving for personal balance and professional growth. I was impressed by her honesty and warmth. How had this preacher's daughter, the youngest of eighteen children, managed to become president of a world-famous company? Her strengths were obvious, but what about her failures and disappointments within corporate America? What was it about her that allowed Candace to continue to strive, despite them?

And I wondered about the politics of race within Soft-Sheen-Carson, a company that is all about "Inspiring Beauty through Innovation for People of Color." Makers of classic name brands such as Dark & Lovely, Care Free Curl, Wave Nouveau (made famous by the jerry curl hairstyle), Optimum Care, and Magic Shaving Powder (a depilatory marketed to black men for prevention of razor bumps since 1901), Soft-Sheen-Carson has its roots in two American family enterprises —one black and one white. Both companies specialized in beauty products for people of African descent, and both are now owned by the French L'Oreal, the largest beauty care company in the world. L'Oreal, in turn, is currently owned by the wealthiest French citizen alive, Liliane Bettencourt.

In the beginning, however, Soft Sheen was a black-owned, family company. It was founded in 1964 by Edward and Bettiann Gardner, who sold homemade hair-care products from their basement on the south side of Chicago. In 1998, the business was purchased by L'Oreal, which currently produces cosmetic product lines such as Lancôme, Maybelline, Garnier, Redken, Kiehl's, Matrix Essentials, La Roche-Posay, Ralph Lauren Fragrances, Giorgio Armani Parfums, Biotherm, and Helena Rubenstein.

In 2000, L'Oreal added the Savannah, Georgia-based Carson Products to its holdings. Carson was formerly held by the Minis family and later DNL Savannah Acquisition Inc. It was a white-owned Southern company that had sold black-oriented beauty products for nearly a century. Its Dark & Lovely no-lye relaxer (the first sodium hydroxide-free formulation) was patented in 1978 by Mario DeLaGuardia who later served as president of Carson from 1982 to 1995.

As I wrote years ago, in a *Washington Post* article about the Rio "natural hair relaxer" scam that resulted in a $500,000 class-action settlement, products that allow African Americans to straighten their hair are of profound cultural importance. They represent in a deeply tangible sense, freedom. Prior to Carson's Dark & Lovely No-Lye Hair Relaxer, black people allowed their scalps to be regularly burned by chemicals to achieve straight hair. Even Malcolm X endured the sizzling pain of relaxers to achieve the flaming hepcat "conk" style of his youth. For many African Americans, both "good hair" and good hair care is tantamount to good character. It matters deeply. Or, to quote a SoftSheen-Carson brochure (which today honors natural styles such as braids and dreadlocks, as well as straight ones, with products such as "Loc & Twist Butter," "Your crown is the root of your aspirations, hopes, life stress, and challenges. When you get your head right the rest follows."

In 2001, SoftSheen-Carson was created as a division within
L'Oreal, and Candace Matthews was appointed its president.
In my time with Candace—over a power lunch at Fresco by
Scotto on Fifty-Second Street, a day in her office, and a visit to
her family's ranch-style home in Westen, Connecticut—I began
to see the world through her eyes. And I began to understand
the profound impact that we could all have, if only we believed
more forcefully, in our own abilities.

* * *

In a small conference room at L'Oreal, Candace met with sales
and marketing teams responsible for accounts in the United
States and the Caribbean. In a far corner of the room, a large
marker board had a few words scribbled in French and English:
to learn/*apprendre*, to speak/*parler*, to understand/*comprendre*.
With 77 percent of L'Oreal's workforce based in France,
someone at SoftSheen-Carson apparently understood that it
would behoove employees to *parlez-vous* at least a little bit. As
she entered the room, Candace, who did not *parlez-vous* much,
carried a small black leather organizer (entries written in
pencil), an eyeglass case, and a Blackberry. She made small talk
briefly with her sing-song sorority voice and then quickly got
down to business.

Amidst a table full of files, sheet protectors, staplers, and calculators, Candace was offered a mock-up for a poster that would later be splattered on highway billboards, city buses, and subways nationwide. The ad was for a new product called "Optimum Oil Therapy" and the design featured a lightly brown-skinned model against a bright canary yellow background. Her windblown hair blew straight upward, in a gravity-defying manner, along with blue-green peacock feathered earrings. Candace reviewed the design in silence before noting that the word 'nurture' was overemphasized. "It's not a selling point," she said. Later, with another product display she would again redirect the team, pointing out wording that was wrongly placed. "I need to see this kind of thing before it goes to print," she explained.

Later, slipping her reading glasses out of their case, Candace used a small plastic ruler to balance her pencil as she underlined line items on a budget sheet. "I'm not paying for those," she snapped, referring to a shipment of defective displays. Her eyes grew wide and her voice adamant. "No way," she repeated. "Not paying for them."

I realized that while there would always be cultural differences among employees around the world, in global corporate finance, it didn't much matter that Candace only knew *un peu* of French. There was one language that was universal: profit and loss. In running her division in the most cost-efficient way, Candace understood the French and the French understood Candace.

But not everyone in the room seemed to get this.

As she spoke, I realized that her tone was remarkably balanced: firm without being angry. "I need you to do XX," she told a voice by speakerphone. "Please let me know how quickly that can be done." Business was not personal. In contrast, one of her employees, a young black woman, had not yet mastered this art of corporate demeanor. Rather than reclining in her chair comfortably and simply absorbing critiques (as did a black male colleague who made casual, nimble calculations on a handheld calculator), her body was tensely rooted in one position as her facial expression, (read "wounded woman") became rigid. "Got it," she would say, far too quickly and curtly, in response to Candace's criticisms. She could not possibly have been listening to what her boss was saying because she was too busy reacting. The mood in the room became tense. I wished I could take the young woman aside and tell her that as little as I knew about corporate America, even I could see that her attitude was all wrong.

* * *

In a private conference for African American female executives at the *Working Mother* conference, I was asked to moderate a discussion. Of the dozen or so women present in my session, most lamented the fact that their executive management teams, composed of mostly white women, fostered "draining work environments." They felt their spirits challenged at every turn. They worried about trying too hard to fit into the cultures of their colleagues. "How do you keep moving ahead," asked one woman with a soft West Indian accent and neat braids pulled into a bun, "without losing a sense of who you are?"

They also wanted to know why white colleagues always saw them as being "angry." They admitted to feeling envy and resentment toward white women who seemed to have "the luxury of always being the revered one." And they hated the way these same women tended to think that black women's problems on the job came "from out of nowhere." "I'm angry," said one, speaking to a hypothetical white female colleague, "because you see me running around here and why can't you just ask if I need help? I've just joined the company, relocated to an all-white suburb. I'm looking for a church for my family and a place to have my hair done. And you say you want to retain people of color and foster more diversity, but you don't act like it. Why can't you ask me if I'm finding everything I need to be comfortable here? Sometimes," she added, "it's just that simple."

When I told her about this scenario at the conference where Candace herself had appeared as a panelist, she agreed that there are still intercultural tensions among employees of different races working together in any corporate environment.

"Like when it comes time for me to get a relaxer," she offered. "[White] people will say, 'Wow, your hair looks great today.' Two weeks later, she continued, they will say, 'Wow, you got your hair cut.' No, I didn't get my hair cut. I just relaxed it and this is what happens when I get it relaxed. You have to take the time to explain."

But she also warned that while there is legitimate anger among African American executives, "I've had to choose when to bring my anger out. It's not a badge that I wear everyday but my colleagues know it's there if it needs to be." She controls her emotions if possible, says Candace, because in this game "attitude makes an enormous difference." So, too, does attire, and overall presentation. "I don't care how anybody else comes to work," she tells young African American employees, "you aren't judged the same way. I see halters. I see skirts that are too short. I see pants that are too tight. If you want to be taken seriously," she tells black women in particular, "you'd better rethink the presentation." "It may not be fair," she adds, "but it's real."

Recalling one colleague in particular who once "had a little attitudinal outburst" at a meeting and slammed her calculator down in Candace's presence, she explains that she called her in to talk to her, not just as her boss, but as a mentor. "I know what it's like to be the one setting the path for others," she says. "And sometimes that means having the hard conversations."

* * *

After graduating from Stanford, Candace's first job was in executive marketing at General Mills in Minneapolis. In many ways it was an ideal beginning for a young black woman. Her first boss was Ann Fudge, the African American powerhouse who would later run Kraft Foods, and who currently serves as chairman and CEO of advertising giant Young & Rubicam Brands. Under Fudge's wing, Candace learned many lessons. She stayed at General Mills for three years even though it was hard being "a single, African American female in Minneapolis, where the winters are long and cold."

Next, Candace made her way to Baltimore to work for Noxell (then parent company of Noxema and CoverGirl). "It was a fun time," she says. "We tested shades for women of color back in 1989," at a time when such a focus was not common within mainstream companies. But the idea was slow to catch on. It had taken years, after all, as Candace points out "for the company to even use a brunette model in its ads rather than a blonde." The rationale was not rooted in a business instinct, she says. Rather, it was "an emotional decision" that came from deep within a culture steeped in traditions of blonde, virginal purity as the ideal image of womanhood. For the time being, CoverGirl remained "blonde hair and blue eyes" and Candace's line sat on a shelf, ignored.

After five years at Noxell, she had only one African American female colleague: her assistant.

From Noxell, Candace moved to Atlanta, Georgia, to take a job in global strategic development at the pharmaceutical firm, Novarta. "I traveled the globe for three years," she says. Australia six times, over a dozen trips to Europe. In one year alone, she went to fourteen different countries. "It was fabulous exposure. No personal life."

Having no personal life was starting to weigh on the thirty-something executive. A few years earlier, she had been hit with tragedy when her closest girlfriend from college and Alpha Kappa Alpha sorority "line sister," Rasheda, died of breast cancer at the age of thirty-two. The loss was shattering, says Candace. But it was also the catalyst that propelled her to make long-overdue changes in her own life. At the time, she says, "I was thirty-three and had been out of business school for eight years. I wasn't starving in any way, shape, or form. And yet, I had been saving every penny I'd ever made, all my life." She didn't take vacations, get manicures, or shop for clothes unless they were on 70 percent discount sale rack. She was forever clipping coupons.

Her friend Rasheda had teased her for years, saying, "You live like you're poor. You're not poor anymore. Go treat yourself to something!" "But I just couldn't," says Candace. "What if the money ran out? I didn't want to be poor again." It was in losing her dear friend that Candace learned a hard lesson: "Life doesn't last forever and you have to start enjoying yourself." She began to take better care of herself, in small ways at first, and by starting a different dialogue with herself. "No, I don't need that," she would say, "but do I deserve to have it? Can I treat myself to something special, every so often?"

As a minister's child, she had been encouraged to play the piano from the time she was six. "We had an upright at home," she says, "but I'd always wanted a baby grand." That year, she got one for the first time. She also had her first home built in Atlanta and began to enjoy some of the finer things in life, such as a cozy fireplace in her bedroom. And while she was thrilled with her professional direction, and beginning to find some balance in her personal life as well, turning thirty-five was torture.

According to her best-laid plans, she had decided to adopt a child if she still found herself single at that age. But when the time came, she couldn't do it. "I realized that fathers are too important." Slowly, the realization dawned on her that she might not become a mother after all. "I wouldn't say that I chose to focus solely on my career all those years," she explains. "I would just say that the balance just never happened earlier. It wasn't that I didn't want it to happen or I excluded it from happening."

She also points out that it was difficult for her to find

African American men who "could deal with my success and independence." By age forty, Candace had begun to make peace with being single. "I was very, very busy," she recalls. Her four-bedroom house was often filled with visiting nieces and nephews; relatives and siblings from Pittsburgh. "I had pretty much resigned myself to it. I said, 'Okay, I'm forty. I'm single. I've never been married. Don't have any children. Oh well, I guess this is what I am destined to do.'" She was content, if that was the word for it. And so she decided to throw herself a lavish, fortieth birthday party.

A week later, she met Bruce.

A Lake Charles, Louisiana native with a deep entrepreneurial streak, like Candace's father, Bruce Matthews, who was then forty as well, owned a coffee shop in Atlanta and also worked in mechanical engineering and construction. "As an entrepreneur," says Candace, "Bruce took a different path in life. That didn't make him any less intelligent. He just took a different path." And yet, she found herself uncomfortable at first with what seemed to be a gaping divide between Bruce's path and her own; her income was stable, while his fluctuated.

Candace sought counseling through couple's ministry at her church. She began to evaluate her own thinking more closely. "Women who are successful want somebody as successful as them," she explains. "But statistically, that's not going to happen for everyone. After I met Bruce and we started going through the premarital counseling, they made me focus on finding what was really important to me. Because you're not going to get it all and sometimes you have to adjust what you're looking for." "Look at the UPS guy. Look at the mailman," agrees Bruce. "You don't know who he is inside. I'm not a doctor or lawyer or Indian chief. I'm Bruce." And Bruce was the right match for Candace. He had a strong personality, a great deal of confidence, and was in no way intimidated by her success. "He's the most secure man I know," she says.

The couple met, counseled, and married within four months.

And now, once again, Candace was ready to set about with a new goal, to have a child. She went through interuterine insemination, fertility drugs, and surgery to remove uterine fibroids—procedures that stretched over a two-year period. "It was just the most horrible thing," she recalls. "It's very invasive, and with the poking and prodding and injections and hormones, and very inanimate. It's hard. You feel like just this vessel." If she didn't conceive by the age of forty-two, she had decided, they would look into adoption. And after three failed attempts at insemination, they did just that. "I was done," recalls Candace. "I said no more."

Unlike her fertility treatments, the adoption process—done through Bethany Christian Services in Atlanta—was relatively painless. "They tell you that you're likely to get a child with issues. And they help you to determine which issues you can handle and which ones you really cannot." Requesting siblings under the age of four, Bruce and Candace were given three-year-old twin girls, Sydney and Simone, within five weeks. "From the day we called, to the day they arrived," says Candace, "five weeks. Unheard of." It was the moment Candace's mother, who had struggled with congestive heart failure over a five-year period, had been waiting for. "She had been saying to me since that past Christmas, that she was just tired," recalls Candace, her eyes becoming teary. "And when we got the girls, in February of 2001, she came down and stayed with us for three weeks. She saw the girls, saw that I was fine, went home, and about three weeks later, she had a heart episode. I honestly believe," she adds, "that she was waiting, because there was no question that I was her baby." Candace's mother died within three months of meeting her grandchildren.

And there was yet another major transition afoot in the Matthews household.

Shortly after Sydney and Simone's arrival, Candace was offered the position as president of SoftSheen-Carson, a major advancement up the corporate ladder that would come with a huge salary increase and a move to Chicago. Candace and Bruce faced a difficult decision.

Their girls had been in three different foster homes and had serious emotional scars. "The first two months they would let out these bloodcurdling screams when it came time to take a bath," says Candace. "They were definitely afraid of the tub and the toilet. Something must have happened to them there, but we don't know what." Their birth mother, who had worked as a prostitute, was determined to be "internally stressed" and the girls, who weighed twenty-six pounds at the age of three, were malnourished and diagnosed with "failure to thrive." "They were very tiny," says Candace. The couple knew that they would need a great deal of personal attention and nurturing to recover.

At the time, Bruce had been thinking about selling his coffee shop, and so,when Candace was offered the job at SoftSheen-Carson, they realized that it made sense for him to become a stay-at-home father. It wasn't easy, they admit. Bruce's manhood was challenged at every turn, as his days began to consist of PTA meetings and carpools to and from school, gymnastics, dance, swimming, and ice-skating lessons. He wrestled with the same constraints that a lot of new mothers feel. "I'm cooped up in the house all day. I don't get to talk to anybody." And he missed the socializing that came with owning a coffee shop (but not the difficulties of managing employees, which he had never enjoyed). But Bruce also had a role model for unconventional parenting: in the 1960s, his own father had raised three children alone "at a time when it was unheard of to be a single father." Today, both Candace and

Bruce agree that it was the right decision. And as for Bruce, he calls himself "the luckiest man in the world." "For hundreds of years," he says, "women have been okay with coming into a husband with a great job. So guess what, it might not be the ideal thing for men, but if it's what we have to do and I'm capable of doing it, I said let's do it. Let's make this family operate."

In fact, I have been surprised recently, by the number of men who are similarly flexible in their relationships with high-powered women. Jenny Alonzo, vice president of Production and Operations Marketing at Lifetime Entertainment, notes that her husband doesn't necessarily "stay home all the time, but he's available all the time" and able to arrange his schedule to pick up their daughters from school. Similarly, Duy-Loan Le, a senior fellow at Texas Instruments, says that even though women are often seen as "second-class citizens in Asian culture," her husband courted her by delivering a cooler of homemade dinner to her workplace lab every Friday night for eight months. "That's how I fell in love with a man," she notes, adding that she and her husband have been married for over twenty-two years.

"Stay-at-home moms have not been given their kudos," offers Bruce. "People have just looked at them as nobody. They don't understand that this job has more emotional demands than any other. You're dealing with the molding and the structuring of a child's life."

Also, as Bruce acknowledges, he has a different temperament than his wife—one that is not necessarily conducive to a corporate environment. "I work well with my hands," he says. "There's nothing I can't fix. I like to build high rises and stadiums. I'm a risk taker and I don't mind opening up businesses from scratch. I don't mind scrimping and saving and working hard. But I'm a worker. There's no way I would make it in corporate America because I'm too rough. And when it's wrong I will let you know. I have no problems standing at my boss's desk and telling him, 'Guess what? Kiss it.'"

Candace, needless to say, is more diplomatic.

For example, when I asked her about the challenges of transitioning a black-owned company to one that is both white and European-owned, she told me that leadership in a family-owned company is more matriarchal or patriarchal, and hence more "directive" in its approach, while employees in large, global corporations have to be "more proactive in their performance. When I pointed out that she hadn't addressed the question of race, Candace explained that she didn't think that race came into play at her company in quite that way. The cultural differences, for example, were more about French versus American. Where the French culture is more "direct and confrontational," she said, American executives tend to be "more polite."

Although she had a public relations office to answer to, I felt it was my responsibility to point out that for many ordinary African Americans, there is in fact a deep sense of sadness that comes with the sale of what is perceived as "our" blood, sweat, and tears to white-owned enterprises. This disappointment has been made clear time and again, with the sales of ventures such as Black Entertainment Television to Viacom, and *Essence* magazine to Time Inc.

When Edward Gardner, a former public-school teacher (described by Candace as "gentle and fatherly") founded Soft Sheen, he was also creating a base for black self-determination in the Black Power era of the 1960s. African Americans, while just 13 percent of the population purchase up to 33 percent of all hair-care products, and many feel that those profits should remain, if possible, in black hands, where people like Edward and Bettiann Gardner have used them to found organizations such as House of Kicks, an indoor amusement park on Chicago's South side, and Black on Black Love, an anti-violence advocacy organization founded after the murder of one of their employees.

But Candace was not able—perhaps understandably—to entertain such thoughts for the record.

According to the Center for Women's Business Research, the number of businesses owned by black women grew 32 percent between 1997 and 2004, while overall female business ownership increased by just 17 percent. While other African

American women may feel that corporate America has no place for them, in the long run, Candace believes that black women can achieve success within corporate America if they chose to do so. For her, it was the choosing that is the key.

I realized as we talked under the covered porch of their Connecticut home—with Candace and I sipping mint tea and Bruce puffing on a Cuban cigar—that Bruce had thought a great deal about what makes a marriage and a family work. It was a topic he and Candace both were happy to expound on.

"I was married to a doctor before," said Bruce. "For her it was all about having big cars and big houses and furniture. I love my ex-wife dearly but I wouldn't want to be married to her because she didn't support me. You know, every man wants a woman who's just going to be behind him and support him. Every man wants that, but no man wants to give that to her. Men have to rethink it," he continued. "There's always a woman throwing dinners and entertaining for successful men. But if you expect a woman to support you for the rest of your life, you have to be there for her. I'm there for Candace because she's there for me."

"When you come home," he said, gesturing across the couple's great lawn toward a large wooden playground where Sydney and Simone, now seven, were playing, "this is your salvation, your haven, your heaven. Hug your wife. Kiss her. Say thank you. Home is not work. Men have to learn to separate those two. Home is bathing a brand-new baby that just came out of .the womb. You don't just toss it up in the air. You're soft with it. You're always minding your p's and q's. That's what home is. You handle home with kid gloves because when the home is happy, your life is fantastic."

* * *

When she arrived at Soft-Sheen/Carson in 2001 Candace brought with her two decades of executive corporate experience from companies like General Mills, Proctor & Gamble, Cover Girl, Bausch & Lomb, and Coca-Cola. She has learned important lessons along the way. She believes that success is about being true to oneself, and not being afraid to verbalize your truth. That's not always easy for women. "If colleagues are scheduling a meeting, you have to be able to say, 'There's a Mother's Day concert at school and I'm the mother. I have to be there." It's about being vocal and upfront about your priorities and totally comfortable with them, rather than lying or trying to figure out how to get out of it. "I don't agree with that," she says, "because I don't believe anybody should compromise who they are for a job."

As for mistakes, there have been those too.

"When I was very, very junior I felt that my work would automatically speak for itself," she says. "I was the ostrich in the sand who thought that you could survive without knowing about the politics going on behind the scenes. But there are games being played all around you. People golfing with each other, aligning with each other and those things really do impact the decisions that are being made. You have to know who is on whose side."

As one senior executive put it to me at the *Working Mother* conference, "In order to advance, you have to let go of some of that private side. You have to take a risk and be vulnerable. Go for that drink after work. If you don't drink, so what. Go and have a ginger ale. When I did it," she continued, "I was shocked to find that I have a lot in common with the white women at my company. We now take turns babysitting for each other. So, go to the office party, even if you are the only black person there. And, yes, it is uncomfortable at first."

Candace, though she has never been one to be found out late at night at the bars and restaurants networking, agrees however that those striving to achieve in a corporate environment must be politically astute. Ann Fudge showed her that she could have a family and a career. "She worked hard," says Candace, "but when it was time to go, she left. And her husband was extremely supportive. At different times, his career even took a backseat, as he did "more entrepreneurial things" to support his wife.

And there are personal considerations to be made, as women

advance and achieve their goals. "I don't want women to think that success doesn't have consequences," says Candace, referring to her difficult infertility treatments. "They may not have been deliberate, or things that you wanted to happen, but they are consequences. I feel very strongly about being honest about that."

Being part of a corporation today is not like it was half a decade ago, when you stayed for life. "Now, it's more like a series of gigs," she says. "You're with a band for this period of time and when that gig is over, you move on. There is always a job out there," she adds. "But it may require a move. And I think for a lot of people, if they're born and bred in a place that they just don't want to leave, their experience will be very different from mine."

There are also major lifestyle adjustments that must be made. As president of SoftSheen-Carson, she went from being a functional head to managing an entire division of a company. "It was a huge leap," she admits, "and there was a lot to learn." And she has been willing to learn and grow at every turn.

And yet even today, she still struggles to take care of herself, both mentally and physically. Over lunch, she confessed that she had not played her beloved piano in six months and she was still trying to find a way to fit exercise into her daily schedule. She admitted to "running herself ragged" as a matter of course. Even today, she says she could never justify buying a pair of Manolo Blahniks, and will perhaps always remains scarred by what she calls a "poverty mentality."

But couples' ministry through her church has at least helped Candace and Bruce to create a balancing source of rejuvenation in their marriage. They taught us to "take fifteen minutes a day, an evening a week, a day a month, and a weekend a quarter." The plan works. On their getaway day, the couple might get in the car and go to Mystic. Last year, they took their first luxury trip ever, chartering a boat to the British Cayman Islands. She has to learn to do this despite her fears about spending money, because the world will "take and take and take" until there's nothing left.

"It's our responsibility," she says, "to draw boundaries for ourselves."

9.

Aspiring sorority member Kristin High with her son, Skyler.

SISTER
Los Angeles, California

O n a Monday night in September just after 10:30 P.M.,
Kristin High and Kenitha Saafir, who were then
twenty-two and twenty-four respectively, and students at California State University Los Angeles, were blindfolded and
driven to the quiet, residential beach of Playa del Rey, where
a few stray boats bobbed in the distance at the marina's
entrance and an American flag rippled in the wind at the
dock's edge. There were two other Alpha Kappa Alpha
sorority hopefuls with them, also blindfolded and dressed
alike, as was the custom in these kinds of outings. Jennifer
Phinsee and Wykida Casey, like Kristina and Kenitha, wore

black running shoes and black sweat suits and did not know where they were being taken. In all, at least eleven women were present on the beach that fateful evening in 2002, members and wannabe members of the citywide Sigma chapter of Alpha Kappa Alpha.

AKA, the nation's first African American sorority, was founded in 1908 by sixteen African American women who attended Howard University. The women aimed to encourage "high scholastic and ethical standards, to promote unity and sisterhood, and to improve the social stature of African Americans." They founded schools, orphanages, senior citizens' homes, political lobbies, research programs for sickle-cell anemia, and the nation's first mobile health clinic. In short, they were about the survival of their people. And so I wondered: when had it lost touch? When had it forgotten its mission?

The surf was unusually rough that night as a result of a hurricane in Mexico, as anyone paying attention to the weather reports would have known. There were fierce riptides and waves breaking as high as ten feet. A lifeguard at Playa who asked not to be identified later explained to me that the ocean floor on that particular beach is geographically unique, in that it quickly drops to a steep incline. "You can get in over your head really quickly," he said. Kristina Anderson, whose home sits at the end of a cul-de-sac on the beach, told me that she saw a "creepy guy" with a shaved head just before 11:30 P.M.

with two African American women in a silver-colored sports utility vehicle with tinted windows. She remembered that one of the women wore long, dark braids and dark sweatpants and didn't look happy. "She had her game face on," she added. "The ocean was ferocious that night," offered Kristina's husband, Hil Anderson. "I'm six feet five and I'd be in over my head from five to ten yards out. Any reasonable person wouldn't have gone anywhere near it."

But this fact apparently didn't trouble the sorority sisters who had organized a "Simon Says" ritual along the shoreline. The blindfolded women were told to do calisthenics on the beach, after which they were led (some say thrown, some say walked willingly) into ocean waters, blindfolded, and with bound hands and feet. If they had survived the outing, Kristin and Kenitha might have boasted to future generations that they pledged "hard" as fraternity and sorority members like to say. They might have even smiled at the memory looking back, had they lived.

But it didn't turn out that way. Shortly before midnight on a beach crowded with ambulances, fire trucks, police squad cars, rescue boats, and a hovering helicopter beaming searchlights, Kristin and Kenitha were pronounced dead at the scene.

Under the California Education Code, "hazing" is defined as "any method of initiation or preinitiation into a student organization . . . which causes, or is likely to cause, bodily danger or physical harm, or personal degradation or disgrace resulting in physical or mental harm." AKA's policy elaborates on this definition to include specific acts of "hitting, striking, laying hands upon, or threatening to do bodily harm," and behavior "causing shame, abuse, insult, humiliation, intimidation, or disgrace." The drowning of Kristin and Kenitha are the first known hazing deaths of black women ever to occur in America.

Both sorority sisters and the pledges Jennifer and Wykida repeated similar, but contradictory stories when questioned. The women had been doing calisthenics along the tide line when a large wave pulled Kenitha in, they said. Since she couldn't swim, Kristin rushed in to save her but was also "overcome by the wave." Others said they went into the water willingly to "rinse off" after exercising—a particularly odd version given that Kristin was pulled from the water still wearing her running shoes.

Kenitha's mother, Janet Martin, a small, delicate woman with smooth, chestnut-brown skin, was first to receive the news. Four months after the drowning of her daughter, I visited her in the Ladera Heights apartment that Kenitha had shared with her husband, Karim Saafir. She wore a slim, mulberry-colored business suit that morning and spoke softly as she recalled how uniformed police officers arrived at her door, and how she had ridden with them in a squad car to deliver the news to Kristin's mother, Reverend Patricia Strong-Fargas, who lived in Compton.

Later that day, surviving pledges Jennifer and Wykida returned Kristin's white Pontiac Sunfire to her mother's home. Tight-lipped and nervous, the women would not speak to Pat Fargas, and stayed in constant cell phone contact with their sorority "big sisters" who were parked just down the street and monitoring their every move. Already, there was a cover-up in the making. According to Kristin's family, several items were missing from her car, including her mandatory AKA pledge journal, referred to by members as "The Brain." Phone numbers of AKA members that had been programmed into her cell phone and two-way pager had all been deleted. Pat Fargas put grieving "on the back burner," she told me. First she needed answers.

Initially, police officers suspected foul play. "Circumstances were unusual," noted the coroner's report. Why would Kristin have willingly walked into the ocean wearing shoes? Almost immediately, Kristin's family slapped the sorority with a $100 million lawsuit naming all of the surviving nine women present on the beach that night: Mitzi Harris, Stephanie McGhee, Taryn Harris, Hollie Foreman, Eboni Stephens, Patience Jordan, Crystal Irby, and pledges Jennifer and Wykida. The lawsuit also named Linda White, then AKA national president, and Diana Shipley, AKA regional director, who were not present on the beach.

National AKA leaders in Chicago shot back terse responses to these charges, claiming that there was no functioning AKA chapter in existence at California State University Los Angeles, and therefore, the organization bore no responsibility for the "accident." In fact, according to Angela Reddock, attorney for Kristin's family, both the address and phone number for the citywide Sigma chapter the women were pledging were removed from AKA's Web site within two weeks of the deaths (the chapter remains officially inactive). This chapter, says Reddock, encompasses several schools throughout the region, including California State Los Angeles. AKA leadership maintained that this chapter "was not authorized to conduct activities in the name of the sorority" and that "to the best of our knowledge, none of the alleged participants on the night in question were active members of AKA." In an official press release, the sorority also offered condolences to both families and promised to "fully cooperate" in any investigation.

"While we understand that the authorities have so far determined that the deaths were accidental," read their four-sentence statement, "the sorority would like to affirm its opposition to any practice or rite that causes or is likely to cause bodily danger, physical harm, or personal degradation or disgrace." (AKA leaders declined to be interviewed for my original report, published in *Essence*.)

* * *

The single-story California ranch home of Reverend Patricia Fargas was alight with Christmas in December of 2002, four months after the loss of her daughter. Inside, there were green and red tablecloths and pinecone and apple centerpieces, a tinsel-covered fir tree, and tall poinsettias tastefully placed throughout her living room, where Pat Fargas greeted me, along with Kristin's fiancé, Holman Arthurs, and the couple's two-year-old son, Skyler.

"From kindergarten, Kristin had always been a great leader," said Pat who, like Janet Martin, also wore a business suit. Both struck me as the kind of mothers who would encourage their daughters to achieve great things. No half-stepping. "She had aims and goals," said Pat. As a teenager, Kristin was the star of all her school plays, a member of the church choir, and a first-string athlete on the school basketball and volleyball teams. She didn't even like volleyball, notes her mother, but she stuck with it "until she could bring home a trophy." Later, as she became politically aware, Kristin marched in rallies protesting police abuse, founded an NAACP chapter on her college campus, and registered black voters in Compton. There was a high school photograph of Kristin receiving first place in a debate competition. And there were trophies. Many, many trophies.

Kristin had several aunts and cousins who had pledged AKA, and she believed that the sorority would open professional doors, said Pat. She wanted to go through it the right way. "She didn't just want to put her name down. Because it is known that if you go through these steps [hazing], sorors in high positions can get you good jobs. People have told us this."

"It does help in terms of certain networks," agrees Deborah Gray White, professor of history at Rutgers University and author of *Too Heavy a Load: Black Women in Defense of Themselves.* "Wherever you go, you can always find an AKA or a Delta and be welcomed." This is critical, she adds, in environments where black women can feel "isolated in particularly vicious ways."

But wouldn't such talented and committed women as Kristin and Kenitha have been successful without the sorority?

"Maybe, and maybe not," offered Kirstin's mother, Pat, who expressed regret at not pledging a sorority herself, during her own college years, because she was raising two daughters. "I've known some people who went to meetings and they were [hurt] because they did not go through the full pledge activities. The positions were not open as well as to the ones who had gone through it. Why do people go for a doctor's degree," she continued, "and they already have a fantastic job? Why do people make a career in the army? For more stripes, more honor. Kristin felt if she could just have this, she would be complete, along with her law degree and everything. Complete."

"Alpha Kappa Alpha Sorority Incorporated has been the only organization that has reigned in my life," wrote Kristin in a personal statement, not long before her death. "The impressions that have been present from strong African American women in my family swayed me in one direction. My desire to become a prominent woman in this society is ever present . . . being that I am a determined, motivated, and conscious person."

That Kristin and Kenitha were active, respectable members of their communities is typical. Had they become AKAs the women would have joined such notable figures as Constance Baker Motley, Toni Morrison, Althea Gibson, Mae Jemison, Suzanne de Passe, Senator Diane Watson, Maya Angelou, Rosa Parks, Ella Fitzgerald, Coretta Scott King, Faye Wattleton, Phylicia Rashad, Jada Pinkett Smith, and thousands of others with ambitious and humanitarian goals.

"I would like to one day open a free health clinic for minority and low income families," writes one AKA member on the organization's Web site. "I am currently the director of the African Education Project," writes another. "All my life," says another, "I have dreamed of helping those who could not help themselves." As AKA President Linda White has noted: "Members have been committed to serving the African American community for more than ninety-five years. We have volunteered in homeless shelters, soup kitchens, detention centers, and much more. We have also taken on a national after-school project dedicated to improving reading skills in children in grades K–3. We have teamed up with the American Cancer Society to fight cancer in the African American community, and we've helped reduce the incidence of sudden infant death syndrome (SIDS) among babies of color. Our contributions are felt in our communities and throughout the world."

During my conversation with Pat Fargas about the merits of AKA membership, Holman Arthurs mostly remained quiet. When he did speak, his voice was reflective and subdued, and the look in his eyes was as though he was just returning from a faraway place. "She was real elegant," he said, when asked to describe Kristin. "Always immaculately dressed and with a beautiful smile. She'd go into a room and talk to everybody." Her character was "always happy, always smiling, always upbeat. Being in love with Kristin was like being a little boy on your birthday. She made you feel special."

And the couple had plans.

In a year, Kristin would graduate with her bachelor's degree in Business Administration while Holman finished his own studies at California State University Dominguez. That summer they would marry, pack up their son, and head for law school on the East Coast, preferably Columbia University or NYU. Kristin, an active member of the NAACP's National Youth Work Committee, would become a civil rights lawyer, said Holman, "fighting for the cause and the community." His role would be to bring in the "big dollars" by practicing entertainment law. "We balanced each other out," he said.

* * *

Across town, in a well-kept apartment on Slauson Avenue near La Cienega, Karim Saafir answered the door wearing a white T-shirt, blue jeans, and large house slippers shaped like bear's feet with long, white claws. "We usually take our shoes off inside," he said quietly. His wife Kenitha was a photographer and artist who had nearly completed her Fine Arts degree. "She called this a self-portrait," said Karim pointing to a surprisingly harrowing portrait of a wild-haired, dreadlocked, fang-toothed woman. The character wore a gold pendant on her forehead and her mouth was stretched wide in a lion's roar. "She wanted to make herself a superhero," he explained. Another, more gentle painting is of a castle and a princess. Kenitha also liked "fairytale Cinderella stories," he said.

Kenitha was strong-willed and tough, said her mother. In

fact, when she was in the sixth grade she physically confronted a white male schoolteacher who made a racist comment. As he talked about his wife, Karim, who is a member of the Alpha Phi Alpha fraternity himself, pressed hard against the left side of his head with one hand. She was tough but she had her weaknesses. She couldn't swim, he explained, and members of the sorority knew that. At one time, she thought about quitting but later changed her mind. Karim had been one of those who originally encouraged his wife to pledge the sorority, but when I asked how he felt about being Greek today he said simply, "I don't know." He said he had lost his best friend. Then he cried. There were no more words. Subsequent calls to Karim's attorney were not returned.

Holman Arthurs is more outspoken about his rage.

"I didn't understand the science," he said angrily. "Okay, we'll have you up late and you have to learn the history, and you get mayonnaise in your hair if you get it wrong and that will teach you humility and get you to bond and that's supposed to teach you about life. But my whole thing was," he continued, "she was working, she was in school, she was the president of the NAACP, she had a child, and she was soon to be married. What more of life do you need to learn?" Pledges were referred to as "Ivys'" (the AKA national symbol) and each one received a little ivy plant, said Holman. "They were supposed to guard the plant with their lives even when people would come up behind them and try to steal it away. It was real foolish stuff." In fact, he says that Kristin too had reached a point where she thought the whole thing "silly." Initially, there had been a fifth pledge that dropped out of the process after the first week. Kristin often wished she had never started. "But since she started," added Holman, "she wanted to finish" and nothing he said could convince her otherwise.

Two days before her death, Kristin's family believes that something went terribly wrong in the pledging process. The women had been taken to Playa del Rey beach the previous Saturday night, a "typical" ritual among fraternities and sororities, say many. When they returned, Pat Fargas recalls that there was a lot of secretive whispering in her house (where Kristin and Skyler lived) and frantic phone calls back and forth. Tensions ran high all weekend, said Holman. He suspects that the pledges had done something wrong—something that deserved "punishment" in the eyes of their sorors. "I think they raised the bar on Monday night when they went back out there."

For months prior to her drowning, Kristin was what Greeks refer to as a "slave," subject to "punishment" at all hours of the night by being made to do manicures, buy and cook food, chauffeur big sisters around town, run errands, and braid hair. Once, recalls Pat Fargas, she came home in the middle of the night covered in green paint. She was profoundly sleep-deprived and at the time of her death had lost close to thirty pounds.

These practices are common during hazing, insiders explain. Mental abuse and physical beatings, also known as paddling, "taking strokes," and "trading wood," are legendary within the Greek system and widely regarded as legitimate tactics to demonstrate one's commitment. According to Lawrence C. Ross, Jr., author of *The Divine Nine: The History of African American Fraternities and Sororities*, a male pledge "puts his right arm to the wall and uses the left to cover his genitalia." He takes his "sado-masochistic" beating, gets back in line, and then comes the next person. The whole idea of a "pledge line" is to teach members "to rely on one another and on Alpha Phi Alpha as a group rather than on oneself as an individual," adds Ross. "That's why you dress alike, act alike, and think alike. By putting people under common pressure you're supposed to share the experience."

But that experience often goes awry.

The widely reported 1989 hazing death of eighteen-year-old Joel Harris, an aspiring Alpha Phi Alpha at Morehouse College who had a known, preexisting heart condition that was exacerbated by blows to his chest, sparked nationwide reforms among black Greek organizations. The following year, the National Pan-Hellenic Council, a coalition of the nine historically African American fraternities and sororities, agreed to "disband pledging as a form of admission" and to institute a new Membership Intake Program (MIP) in its place. In their formal resolution, the Council prohibited "paddling, creation of excessive fatigue, physical or psychological shock, morally degrading or humiliating activities [or] late work sessions that interfere with scholastic activities." Hazing was "not a requirement for membership," they insisted, "nor is it tolerated."

Such reforms have had little impact however, says Lawrence Ross. New members are asked, "Pledge or paper?" Their meaning is clear. They want to know, "Are you for real, or did you 'skate'?" This is what Pat Fargas meant when she said that Kristin wanted to do it the "right way." When members slip in without really "pledging hard," they're accused of being "T-shirt wearers" and phonies. Some have literally had their Greek-letter shirts ripped from their backs at official events by allegedly "legitimate" members. Anyone who doesn't go through hazing can expect to be "harassed and ridiculed far worse than anything he or she would receive while on line," said one member of a Greek organization who asked not to be named in this story. You will be "outcast and shunned in public," she said. "Followed and constantly taunted."

And so, local chapters continue to engage in the underground process. In the wake of so many lawsuits, says Ross, some pledges have even been instructed to beat themselves, to avoid legal liability in the event of death or hospitalization.

One former student at California State University Northridge recalls a horrific pledge process that lasted over a year. Now a fifth-grade schoolteacher, she did not want her name used, even today, for fear of retaliation by her sorors.

It works like this, she explained:

"You get an invitation to come over . . . the whole thing seems friendly and innocent in the beginning. They call these events 'icebreakers.'" At first, the chores she was given were fairly lightweight: community service and posting signs. But before long, this pledge who we'll call Jackie was being asked to buy gifts and meals for her AKA sisters that came to a bill of nearly $400 over a three-month period. When her group of pledges refused to pay for the dinners of twelve big sisters one evening, things got ugly. One pledge (not Jackie, she says) reported the hazing activities to the sorority's regional director and the chapter was suspended from campus. Then began the death threats to all of the pledges in her group: constant, anonymous calls at all hours of the night. Jackie also had to pay for $1,200 worth of damages to her new car. Suffering from nervous tension and stress, she withdrew her enrollment from CSUN, moved out of her apartment, and returned to her parents' home.

This particularly brutal chapter at California State

Northridge liked to refer to themselves as "Death Row," she explained. Once, Jackie was forced to drive a group of big sisters from the San Fernando Valley to Compton which was seventy miles away, during which time she also had to answer a barrage of history questions. When her answers didn't meet the satisfaction of her sorors, she was ordered to pull over on the freeway and to get out of the car during a rainstorm. "Pull down your pants," one soror demanded. "You're gonna take some wood right now!"

But the worst night, recalled Jackie, was when she witnessed a five-year-old girl (the daughter of a big sister) being placed in charge of paddling. "You walked in," she said, "and this little girl would yell, 'Get in the cut!' with her mother standing right there watching. Her attitude was, 'My momma does it.'" Furthermore, several of the bisexual sorors wanted sexual favors. "These weren't ladies," she said. "These were gang members." But it wasn't until years later that Jackie would learn just how common such violence was. "I found out my uncle had kidney problems after he pledged," she says (a common complication of repeated beatings). And she learned that a girlfriend had been punched in the face by her big sisters and given a black eye.

Another woman interviewed told me about a close friend who went away to a historically black college as an "intelligent and composed" young woman, and returned home a "squeaking, stepping fool." During her hazing, says this source who also did not wish to be named, her friend ate raw onions and eggs until she vomited and allowed sorority sisters to "beat the crap out of her in a darkened room with her eyes blindfolded."

Official medical reports of alleged hazing incidents are typical: "broken jaw," "blood clot in spleen," "liver damage," "ruptured ear drum," "severely infected buttocks requiring surgery," "abdominal injuries from being stood on," "torn blood vessels from being paddled seventy times," "kidney dialysis machine after beaten with a paddle and cane," "concussion and cigarette burns," "hospitalized, broken ribs, injured kidneys, face, neck, and chest," "pushed through a wall," "surgery for infections on buttocks," "colostomy performed," "serious injuries to stomach, blood in urine," "torn skin on lower back and buttocks," "internal bleeding and lost consciousness," "punctured lung from chest punches," "paddling wound seven inches round and half-inch deep, requiring two surgeries including skin graft . . . "

Even scholar Paula Giddings writes in the preface to her book *In Search of Sisterhood* (a largely celebratory history of the Delta Sigma Theta) that many see hazing as "the downside" of sorority life. "A paddling incident during my own pledge period," she offers somewhat cryptically, "cast a shadow over the whole sorority experience. It was one of the reasons why I ceased to be an active member or join any of the alumnae groups after I graduated."

And yet, many defend hazing as a necessary ritual to teach sacrifice and loyalty, comparing the pledge process to socially and legally sanctioned boot camp training in the military. "Over 95 percent of all black leaders in the twentieth century belonged to black Greek lettered organizations," wrote a member on an online message board. "Thurgood Marshall, Dr. Martin Luther King, Jr., Andrew Young, Bill Cosby, Michael Jordan, Dick Gregory, Arthur Ashe. . . . If hazing is so bad, then how is it that most of [them] made it through? They got their asses kicked just like others."

"It's Egyptology," explained Russell Rickford, a proud Alpha Phi Alpha and author of *Betty Shabaaz: Her Life with Malcolm X and Fight to Preserve His Legacy.* "The thinking is that in the ancient mystery schools in Kemet, young initiates had to undergo a number of trials to prove themselves worthy. You didn't just become eighteen and suddenly you were an adult. One had to prove oneself. In the 1960s when black Americans started embracing Africa," continued Rickford who also holds a Master of Arts in African American Studies from Columbia University, "this thinking became very prevalent. It's the notion that one has to be broken down before one is built back up. Critics always talk about how pledging mirrors slavery," he adds. "But what's interesting is that the same analogy is made from within the organizations in a positive way. They say, 'This beating is connecting you to your ancestors.'"

"That's the most ridiculous thing I ever heard," offered historian Deborah Gray White. "If our ancestors heard that they'd be turning over in their graves."

In talking with Greeks like Rickford, who I consider a friend, I heard both admiration and disgust for hazing practices. "The Afrocentric argument is problematic," he admitted, "in that it presents an archaic understanding of African cultures that reifies old pathologies." On the other hand, he offered, spinning in the opposite direction as a loyal fraternity member himself, "I've met brothas from the 1940s who went through these practices, and I would be dishonest if I didn't say that there was a kind of respect for them. It's empowering to know that you've shared that experience."

In fact, even Jackie, who was so traumatized by her experience at California State Northridge, stuck with the sorority and eventually pledged. "My aunt and grandmother were AKAs," she explains. And when it was all over, a sorority sister offered her a job "no questions asked," without even bothering to interview her.

When asked if he regretted his own pledging days, Russell Rickford smiled and shook his head. "It taught me how to be intimate with black men. How to say I love you and not be ashamed. And it gave me friends for life. I'm very grateful for that. I mean this is something you're doing for life. And some believe, beyond life."

Now, beyond life is all Holman Arthurs has.

In April of 2005, the lawsuit filed against AKA on behalf of Kristin High was settled for an undisclosed sum and the organization committed to a number of reforms such as clearer notification of suspended chapters. But Kristin's family was not satisfied with the results and many of the reforms have yet to be put into effect. "There were so many lies told," said Pat Fargas. "The sorority did not in the end live up to its promise to publicize the need for better policing of hazing. Everything was just brushed under the rug."

In fact, as recently as September of 2005, the *St. Louis Post Dispatch* reported that a former St. Louis University student, Courtney Easter, had also filed suit against AKA for its role in an October 2003 car accident involving a group of sleep-deprived sorority initiates who had been forced to stay awake over a five-night period. All four of the women in the car, including the driver, fell asleep on their way to classes early in the evening and Easter had reportedly suffered severe injuries, including brain damage. According to the *Post Dispatch*, representatives at the sorority's headquarters in Chicago did not return calls for comment at press time, and had not taken any responsibility for the accident.

Because Kristin and Kenitha's case was settled out of court, none of the women present at Playa del Rey beach on that fateful evening of September 9, 2002, were ever required to take the stand, or even to explain their actions publicly. No criminal action was taken against them, and they were allowed to essentially "disappear" back into their private lives.

In the weeks and months after his mother's death, Skyler was inconsolable. Often, he begged Holman to take off his shirt or lift his sleeve, so that he could "kiss Mommy" (an image of Kristin tattooed on Holman's upper arm). He cried all the time, says Holman. Even today, at five, their son—who attends the Ruby Christian Academy, a school owned by Pat Fargas's family, and now lives with Holman—is still trying to make sense of that fateful night. "Why was Mommy in the water?" he'll ask. "And sometimes he just gets real whiny," says Holman, now twenty-eight. "And I realize that he's missing his mom and I just gotta sit down and hug him."

In the spring of 2002, Holman completed his undergraduate degree from California State Dominguez on schedule, magna cum laude with a 3.85 grade point average, the highest in his class. The following year he received a Master of Arts degree in sociology. "It's not how I thought the cards would be dealt," he explained when I asked how he has held it all together these past few years. "But I have a son and I have to be strong for him. For the beautiful baby boy that we made together." Today Holman works as a sociologist and senior community health researcher at Charles Drew University of Medicine and Science in Compton, and says that next year he plans to attend law school at the University of Southern California or the University of California Los Angeles. His mother, a retired nurse from Brooklyn, New York, has since moved to Los Angeles to help raise Skyler.

Recently Holman recorded a rap song with some Southern artists in Atlanta about Kristin's death. He also planned to make a documentary film, so that people would know all about Kristin and the problem of hazing. "I was heavily into entertainment before," he said, noting that he worked with rappers while pursuing his undergraduate studies. Now for the first time in years, he was ready to "get back in the game." Recording a song he wrote called "Don't Understand the Pain" was kind of like a "little therapy session," he said. "Kristin was the only girlfriend I ever really had, the only one I ever introduced to my family. And she died, just to be sisters with those women."

"But that was no type of sisterhood."

10.

A woman meditates.

PRISONER
Seattle, Washington

A t the North Rehabilitation Facility in Seattle, the image
of Marilyn Ann West haunted me. Smoking a hand-
rolled cigarette in the enclosed yard of the women's dorm,
she was tall and big-boned and wore her hair in thick, no-
nonsense cornrows. Looked like she could pop a cap in
someone's ass, I thought. She seemed to belong in a maximum-
security facility instead of here. But I misread Marilyn. I took
her surly silence for hostility, when the truth was that Marilyn
rarely smiled because she was ashamed. An abusive pimp had
permanently bruised her gums and left her with several
missing front teeth. When she did allow herself a grin, it came

across as girlish and shy, one hand covering her mouth in embarrassment.

Marilyn, like the majority of black women housed in the minimum-security prison, was a drug addict, an alcoholic, and a prostitute sentenced on nonviolent, drug-related offenses. At forty, she was older than most of the women there, but somehow more vulnerable, too. "I've been alcoholic since twelve," she wrote in a handwritten, autobiographical letter. She wanted to get her thoughts down before speaking with me, she said. She wanted "to make sure she got it right."

"Drugs since twenty-four," continued the pencil scribbling on the page. "I used to skip school and drink from a bottle my mom used to keep in a bar tray for her company. . . . Ran away when I was twelve and got into trouble . . . got locked up until I was fifteen. Got out went back to my mom and started drinking again. Left and got with this man name Harold. He was forty-five and my mom was really mad but I didn't care at the time." At seventeen, Marilyn met her first husband who was also a pimp. With him she "started hoeing and taking speed, weed, and pills," as she puts it. "It was a good marriage," she wrote, "until he killed his mistress."

The rate of imprisonment for American women increased by 460 percent from 1980 to 1995, according to The Sentencing Project in Washington, D.C. For women of color that figure was 500 percent. For African American women, the fastest growing prison population of all, it leapt to over 800 percent, or seven times the rate of incarceration for Caucasian women. And, of course, the vast majority of black women doing time are in for drug-related offenses. They are addicts and dealers or they are in love with addicts and dealers. And this life, the criminal underground economy, is often the only one they know.

Like Marilyn, most black women serving time in prison have also been sexually and/or physically abused as children and/or as adults, a fact that many treatment programs fail to address. And, of course, the incidents of violence in black women's lives—sexual assaults, domestic violence, and homicide—are higher by any measure than those of women of other races, even given the fact that black women are less likely to report crimes committed against them by African American men. It is important to note here that one of the major indicators of these disproportionate numbers is, in fact, not race, but economic status. It is *poor* and *unemployed* men of all races who are more likely to commit acts of violence against women. But because black men happen to be disproportionately under employed and members of the so-called permanent underclass, the racial statistics read the way they do.

The links between past acts of violence against women and girls and present incarceration are so clear that it is maddening.

According to the National Institute of Justice, abuse during childhood increases the likelihood of juvenile arrest by 53 percent. For adult *women* who are abused or neglected in childhood, however, the likelihood of arrest leaps by 77 percent. Moreover, Columbia University's National Center on Addiction and Substance Abuse has found that the children of drug-addicted and alcoholic parents are almost three times more likely to be abused and more than four times likelier to be neglected than other children. At North Rehabilitation Facility (NRF) 90 percent of the female inmates were addicts, while nationwide, about 80 percent of women in state prisons have substance abuse problems. And, yet, across this country only a fraction of such traumatized women (10 to 20 percent) receive treatment while doing time.

Why?

I went to NRF, not because it had a large number of black female inmates (25 percent) but because, of all the prisons in America, it offered women of all races something other than punishment for their pain. It offered a radical and exciting experiment in rehabilitation.

Through a cooperative effort between Seattle's King County Correctional System and the Department of Public Health, NRF, with a population of just under three hundred adult men and women, experimented with innovative healing strategies for drug and alcohol abuse such as acupuncture, yoga, Tai

Chi, and meditation. Meditation has long been proven by neurobiologists to increase activity in the prefrontal cortex region of the brain, an area strongly associated with emotional well-being. In addition to some of the usual programs and classes in critical thinking, anger management, and parenting skills, NRF provided dormlike facilities instead of cells, and referred to its population as "residents" rather than inmates. There was no slamming of iron doors at NRF. Residents, none of whom were convicted on violent felony charges or sex offenses, were free to roam the grounds as they pleased, returning to their rooms frequently for head counts.

As Prison Administrator Lucia Meijer put it to me, NRF was "trying to shake loose the old ideas of what you can and can't do with inmates." And, so, in October of 1997, under Meijer's leadership, NRF, a deteriorated and somewhat forgotten facility housed in pre–World War II hospital barracks, became the first United States prison to implement a ten-day course in complete silence and Vipassana meditation. Between 1997 and 2002, a total of twenty additional courses were completed by 130 men and 61 women—(22 percent of those who began the course dropped out)—many of the men with histories of domestic violence and assault and most men and women serving time on felony property and drug-related crimes.

The word "Vipassana" from the Pali language, means "insight" or "to see things as they really are." Over twenty-five hundred years old, Vipassana meditation was a "mental discipline and ethical practice taught by the historic Buddha," according to Lucia Meijer. "Although it contains the core of what later has been called Buddhism," she writes in an article for *American Jails*, "it is not an organized religion, requires no conversion, and is practiced by people of many different faiths and nationalities."

First instituted as a means for prisoner reform in Jaipur, India, in 1975, Vipassana was resurrected nearly two decades later, most famously at the New Delhi Tihar Prison in 1994, one of India's most violent facilities, by the country's first female police officer, Kiran Bedi. The course has been described as a success by officials there for the over one thousand inmates who participated. Tihar now has a permanent mediation center within the prison and the course is offered in facilities throughout the country, as well as in Taiwan. The story of Tihar's Vipassana program is documented in the 1997 film *Doing Time, Doing Vipassana.*

After hearing about the impact of the program in other countries, Lucia Meijer was inspired by its potential to help residents at NRF. Having no real understanding of how Vipassana worked however, she decided to complete a ten-day course herself before approving the program. "I thought it would be a nice vacation," said Meijer, who was Caucasian, with shoulder-length gray hair. She spoke with the cool authority you might expect from a government administrator. Her tone maintained professional distance, but her words revealed the depth of her personal experience. She found that being isolated for ten days in "noble silence" without any kind of physical or even eye contact turned out to be quite an ordeal.

"A very deep and difficult journey," as she put it. Somewhere in the distance, the smell of incense wafted through her office window as I digested her words in silence.

NRF Programs Manager David Murphy, a Caucasian man of average build with salt-and-pepper wavy hair, also took a course in Vipassana in order to help determine its potential impact on residents. In talking with Murphy I found him to be, like Meijer, deeply moved by the experience. At times during the course, he endured painful emotional "storms" as they call them, triggered by a wild unleashing of unconscious thoughts. These could be random recollections of jingles, song lyrics, memories, and bits of conversation, anything really. They came "from out of nowhere" and overwhelmed him. Murphy saw clearly the chaos in his mind and body during these storms. "I would be thinking about my wife, my mortgage payment, a talk I was going to give . . . and then as I got deeper into the meditation, childhood issues with my parents, my siblings, being embarrassed at school. I saw that all of these old feelings were still very much alive within me."

The second time he took the course, the storms were even more intense. Like a deeper incision during a critical surgery. "I wanted to leave on day five," he recalls.

But then, Murphy experienced a storm in which he recalled an old television commercial that had featured a famous basketball star. In it, the camera starts at his feet and slowly pans up his entire seven-foot-tall body to his head, as the imposing athlete leans forward and peers directly into the camera, asking, "How does it feel when I get in your face?" For Murphy, the image took on new meaning as he relived long-forgotten interactions with his ten-year-old son, in which he had been just as overbearing. "I thought this poor kid who is, you know, a third of my size. And when I got mad at my own stuff, at work or whatever, I was reacting by taking it out on him, and bringing him to tears. I'm not proud of that," he adds. The connection between the image and his own past behavior shook Murphy to his core and gave him a profound new insight into the vulnerability of children. The experience, he said, revolutionized his parenting.

Vipassana meditation is thought to be ideal for people battling substance addictions, and with cognitive impairment as a result of their habits. As Meijer put it, it is an "acutely uncomfortable form of mental detox for folks who literally can't think straight." During the course students are taught both to "calm and focus the mind and to train it to systematically observe [the physical body, emotions, and thoughts] without clinging or craving" and without "fear or aversion." As instructor Rick Crutcher explained, "The mind is angry. The mind is frustrated. The mind is bored. Vipassana is the process of starting over again and again, and facing the mind." The concept of *anicha* kicks in, they say: a Pali word that means, "Nothing's permanent. Everything passes."

It's like an evaporative process, continued Crutcher. If an emotion or thought is allowed to simply keep "bubbling up and bubbling up" without being suppressed with drugs or lies, it will eventually dissipate. The storms can be "images, thoughts, words, or feelings." "You don't know why you're so wound up, or on edge . . . because it's coming from a much deeper level than the rational mind, through the sensations of the body." Vipassana "works at that very deep, primordial level of craving," he concluded. It teaches us that "suffering exists. Suffering is. But we can go beyond it."

The first session begins at 4:30 A.M. and the last ends at 9:30 P.M. Other than short breaks for meals and showers, no other activities are allowed throughout the ten-day, eleven-night course. There is no smoking, television, reading, knitting, writing, or conversation for ten days: just the constant and relentless observation of one's own breathing. Participants are also required to commit to a code of moral conduct whereby they agree not to kill (not even a fly), lie, steal, engage in sexual misconduct, or use intoxicants.

The start-up cost for the program at NRF was about $1,500, which was used to renovate a separate dorm area for participants. Teachers served on a volunteer basis and mats and other materials were donated. For Meijer, such miniscule figures were weighed against the cost of housing repeat offenders. In some states, it is estimated that taxpayers save $7.14 in future incarceration costs for every $1.00 invested in treatment.

"Most people in the criminal justice field get excited when you talk about even a 5 percent reduction in recidivism," explained Meijer. Residents participating in the meditation program at NRF showed a 20 to 25 percent decrease in their rate of return to prison, according to studies completed by both NRF and the University of Washington. The course also impacted inmate behavior. Those who completed it became more cooperative and got along better with other inmates. According to the University of Washington study, they also had reductions in "drug use, anxiety, depression, and hostility."

* * *

Folding chairs inside NRF's dilapidated gymnasium were set up for visiting family members, guests, and inmates to celebrate a group of female Vipassana students' successful completion of the course. A modest table offering included coffee, tea, and pastries as a white woman in her early thirties, whose name was not given for the record, took the podium. Describing herself as an alcoholic and drug addict, she said that the process of "sitting the course" for ten days made her feel "really proud, and peaceful. I realized that I never cried before," she explained, "and now I couldn't stop. It kind of dawned on me that the iceberg over my emotions was being melted. And I felt like . . . it was gonna be okay. There were times when I wanted to leave, but I'm glad I didn't. The course teaches you to go down really deep inside and see what's there. I feel very lucky. Thank you."

Vipassana seemed so promising. But there was a catch. Most of the black women at NRF weren't interested.

Here in the Seattle area, explained Meijer, there was a relatively large population of Native American women. This demographic has found Vipassana to be "highly compatible with the spiritual practices of their homes," she said. "Women from Christian backgrounds, on the other hand, have found the idea disturbing. So there are some real cultural issues." To add to the divide, Bible-study volunteers who visited the facility on a regular basis surprised Meijer by coming out strongly against the meditation practice and advising Christian women (many of them African American) that it was equivalent to "devil-worship." While their work has been "wonderful and much appreciated," said Meijer, she was also torn by the impact they were having on women in need of substance abuse treatment.

But there were African Americans who embraced the practice. During my visit to Seattle, I met with Richard Jimerson, thirty-six, an unassuming man who wore bottle-thick prescription eyeglasses and spoke so softly it was difficult to hear him. Jimerson had arrived at NRF with forty-five prior arrests in King County, he told me as we sat in his mother's home eating natural cookies and drinking tea. He had done time on charges ranging from driving under the influence to theft, and although he had tried twelve-step programs and church nothing worked. Glancing at the walls in Mrs. Jimerson's home, I noticed a prominent trinity of images over the mantle: Malcolm X, Martin Luther King, Jr., and Nelson Mandela.

In 1997, Richard sat at the first Vipassana meditation course ever to be held at NRF. Three months later, he was released. Over a year later, he still had not returned, much to his mother's surprise. In fact, Mrs. Hilliard Jimerson was so stunned by the changes in her son that she too decided to take a course in Vipassana at a local nonprison center in Ethel, Washington.

In her work at a security desk for AT&T, she often did double shifts, starting her day at 4:00 A.M. and returning home after 8:00 P.M. in the evening. "A long, weary day," as she put it. She found that the breathing techniques of Vipassana "kind of simmers me down when I'm distressed or stressed out." In Ethel, she recalls sitting in a dining hall at sunrise, after the day's first meditation and looking out the room's large picture windows. "It was so still in there, you could hear a pin fall," she said. "And a beautiful, magnificent burst just zipped over me! As I looked out, I thought, 'Isn't it wonderful? The power of God?'"

"My wisdom comes from the Bible," she offered when I asked if she thought the practice conflicted with her Christianity. Meditation, she said, is nothing more than "a supreme feeling of peace." It's a feeling that can come through prayer or meditation, or both. "Now, I don't know no other way to describe it," she added emphatically. "I say the spirit of God is *everywhere* you go."

* * *

In a tiny room at North Rehabilitation Facility, used for Narcotics Anonymous meetings and Bible study, a handful of black women residents were eager to share their stories with me. Marilyn, Marlene, Florence, and Monica each identified themselves as Christians. None had tried Vipassana meditation. Unsolicited, Marilyn offered me the five pages of notes she had scribbled out during lunch. Now, she took the sheets, which had been twisted into a roll, and smoothed them onto the table. This was Marilyn's story, quoted in full.

"My name is Marilyn Ann West. I'm an alcoholic and addict. I've been alcoholic since twelve. Drugs twenty-four. I started drinking from 'clean up' parties my brother and sister and I had after my parent's parties. I used to skip school and drink from a bottle my mom used to keep in a bar tray for her company and put water in it so she wouldn't know. I would also go in her drawer and get cigarettes . . . started drinking and smoking pot sex teenage girls always go crazy after sex so I left got with this man name Harold he was forty-five at the time. . . . Moved in with him and messed up for real...

"Started going to taverns, panhandling, drinking T-bird behind Safeway by Holly Park. His older friend would try to molest me when I would pass out. I would wake up fighting him off . . . got tired of that not knowing if it was night or day . . . so I went back home and was expected to go to school and straighten out. I did for a while and I met my first husband Donald . . . started hoeing and taking speed everything was cool, married my pimp in 1979, five days after my eighteenth birthday. We moved to Atlanta I stopped hoeing because he told me he would kill me if I didn't. Huh? So he got a job and so did I. We had a good marriage until he killed his mistress.

"I moved to Washington, D.C., hoeing again for another pimp more pills he had two white girls also but I ran them off and then I left him and was working for myself. I was there for seven months but I had my nineteenth birthday got drunk and this girl's boyfriend got fresh and I told him no . . . his girlfriend came up behind me with a broken bottle hit me in the head. I got off the street for a while got a job met a nice guy started shooting dope after about three months of that he sent me home he knew I wasn't happy so I came back to crack and a man I've been knowing since before I ever left in the first place."

What did she want to do when she got out of NRF? I asked Marilyn.

Her plan was to stay in a hotel room that her "sugar daddy" has promised to pay for. "We're just friends though," she added, saying he didn't want anything from her. For a moment, we were both silent. When I asked if she had any hopes or dreams for her future, Marilyn thought for a moment and then told me that she really wants to "get on one of them boats" operated by Alaskan fishing companies. The jobs pay up to $5,000 a month for workers who sign a three- to six-month contract for hard physical labor at sea. They have to pass a drug test though. Marilyn thought the job might help her stay clean. She needed a change, she said. She needed to get away. She didn't know where to begin.

On another day, I was talking to Marilyn in the office of a NRF staff member, when I noticed among the scattered photocopies of housing applications, GED program applications, and addresses for churches and outreach programs, a single sheet of paper that somehow stood apart from all the others. There was only one like it, and no other copies anywhere. On it were the names and numbers for forty-five fishing boat companies hiring year round. I gave it to Marilyn, who smiled bashfully, not showing her teeth, and tucked the paper away in a pocket.

The women wanted to be heard, wanted their stories known. They talked for hours. Florence, nineteen, was locked up because a boyfriend (she never knew his last name) convinced her to deposit a $9,000 forged check into her bank account. Both were convicted of felonies. Monica, twenty-two, had left her home in Texas after learning that her father was a drug addict. She partnered with a "big time" drug dealer, as she put it, upon arriving in Seattle and in three years time had racked up four felonies.

Marlene, thirty, was a crack addict still trying to gain her mother's love and the approval of her nine siblings, including brothers who sexually molested her as a child. When one of her brothers was thirteen and she was four, he "used to make me go down on him," she said. "He'd tell me if I didn't do it right, he would beat me. My mama would always leave at night to go party, and he'd tell me I wasn't gonna eat if I didn't do it. He used to make me clean his room too," she adds, "and he'd come in the room and hump me."

Another brother also fondled her while her mother was out. And a third, who later died of AIDS, forced Marlene to have sex with him in exchange for food. "I was hungry," she said with an incongruous laugh, as though adding a punch line to a joke.

"So I would say, "Okay, give me the food first! It wasn't as bad with him as it was with the other two.""

Marlene's father, an alcoholic and crack addict, was also in prison at that very moment for "burning up his girlfriend's face." He wasn't around much when she was a girl, and when he was, she spent a lot of her time defending her mother from his blows. "I was always standing in the middle of fights," she recalls adding, "Yeah, he hit me, too. But I'm here." When asked to explain her mother's neglect, Marlene describes her mother as "an innocent gal" who was without a mother herself. "And she was abused and stuff. She'd been to prison, too, cuz she ended up killing a lady. But she didn't mean to. She was defending the guy she went out to the bar with. The gal said something and my mother hit her over the head and it just killed her."

At eighteen, Marlene smoked crack cocaine for the first time. By her fourth hit, she says, she was addicted—"pulling her hair out" in need of more. She did it to be closer to the father of her child. "I thought it would help the relationship grow." Instead, the couple, who now have three children together, all of them in foster care, both ended up at NRF: he in the men's section and she in the women's.

A month after leaving NRF (her sentence was minimal, as were those of most inmates doing time at the facility), Marlene surprised me with a phone call to let me know how she was doing. She was staying at her mother's house with most of her brothers, whom she was still afraid to look in the eye. So far, she had not relapsed into drugs. "I'm not gonna lie. I have a few beers," she said. "But I'm trying to just take things nice and slow." Through a NRF training program she had been certified as a "road flagger" for the state, but had not yet been assigned to a job. She was anxious to get out of the house, she said.

She could have gone to a Narcotics Anonymous meeting and gotten a sponsor, like she had planned to do when she was locked up, I offered. She could have even applied for transitional housing and counseling, like she had also promised. But she did neither. I was not hopeful about her future. She seemed agitated and hyped. And the very fact that she had returned to her mother's home to live with her brothers spoke volumes about her mental health. I wondered what might have happened if she had tried Vipassana's process of looking at the mind, and what she might have found there.

I wondered if, instead of a pimp's hotel room, Marilyn might have made it out on the healing waters of the ocean, had she faced the interiors of her body for ten days.

But then again, as Meijer admitted, "Vipassana is not a magic pill."

Among the very few African American women who had participated in the program, recidivism rates, oddly, had not improved. "Those women came from and went back to very hostile environments," explained Meijer. "Hostile to quality of life . . . hostile to hope. They had been programmed for failure from a very early point in their lives." Vipassana is "an individual journey," she concluded. Not everyone travels to the same end.

In 1999, two years after Vipassana was implemented at NRF, the facility was one of nine jails and prisons listed by the U.S. Department of Health and Human Services as offering promise in substance abuse treatment. Because of its success, the program was also implemented in facilities throughout the country; thirteen inmates completed the program in a San Francisco, California, jail in 2001 and a maximum security prison in Bessemer, Alabama, provided thirty-eight men, many of them serving life sentences, with the program in 2002. Among administrators in various states there was talk of bringing the program to New Mexico, Texas, Massachusetts, and Vermont. But so far neither Alabama nor California are pursuing their programs and none of the rumored courses in other states have materialized—although one is reportedly still in the planning stages at the Dale Correctional Facility for women in Waterbury, Vermont.

It has always fascinated me that there are eleven definitions of justice in the *Black's Law Dictionary*. There is distributive justice, or that which is thought to be "owed to a community" and which includes "the fair disbursement of common advantages and the sharing of common burdens." There is natural justice, which is defined "in a moral as opposed to a legal sense." There is social justice, one of my favorites, that conforms to a similar moral principle as well, for all people. And then there is the concept of popular justice, which we might say is that most commonly applied to the criminal-justice system in America: a simplified form, according to *Black's*, that is "usually considered less than fully fair and proper even though it satisfies prevailing public opinion in a particular case."

In the late 1990s, executive administrators for King County suggested, oddly, that the facility, which was desperately in need of $20 million in renovation funds, might continue to operate as a mere jail without rehabilitative programs. Lucia Meijer and David Murphy both refused to be a part of such a program, protesting that such a move would make NRF nothing more than just another holding pen without hope. "I have searched my entire professional career to feel a part of something that's really making a difference," explained Murphy. "We have a very narrow window of opportunity here to educate the public and the taxpayers. If this institution shuts down," he added, "it won't happen again."

North Rehabilitation Facility in Seattle, Washington closed its doors in November 2002 due to state budget cuts.

The author surveying a vegetable garden in Pine Bluff,
Arkansas, with her cousin Laura Hunter.

EPILOGUE

J ust south of Pine Bluff, up a long, red clay dirt road, at the top of a shady hill in Tarry, Arkansas, there was once a large plantation-style home that belonged to a white man named Horace Brent and his sister. Nearby, in a small cabin lived my great grandmother, a black woman named Delphine. At least we think that is her name. Delphine gave birth to two biracial sons by Horace. One of them, Arthur, left Arkansas as a teenager and moved to Chicago, where he married my grandmother, Christine, when she was just sixteen. Arthur and Christine's families knew each other from neighboring Moscow, where my grandmother spent the first eight years of her life.

At the intersection where the roads to Moscow and Tarry meet, there are 140 acres of land still in our family's name, managed by our cousin, Clem Hunter, who is now sixty-two. There were once seven brothers to inherit and farm the land, Clem tells us. Some of them left for cities like New Orleans, where they were killed in drug-related incidents. And so, the land sits abandoned today, covered with rusty tractors because no one wants it. "What would they do with it?" they say, as if farming were some ancient way of life from a prehistoric universe. But Clem remembers. He used to walk down the same road my grandmother walked, for fresh buttermilk from Big Ma's farm. Along the way he picked plums on the side of the road, blueberries and apples, peaches and pears. Now there are commercial soybean crops and rice as far as the eye can see.

Our cousin Laura Hunter, who is thirty-nine like me, tells us that as a girl she shelled purple hull peas on the family porch with her siblings for a $2.00 allowance. Her mother, who died just last year from diabetes, was a proud homemaker who cooked three hot meals for her family, every day of the week. Laura says this with tears in her eyes because she misses her still. Laura's father, Melvin, grew up in a house next to the Old Morning Star Missionary Baptist Church in Pine Bluff, where his brother is now a preacher. When we visit Cousin Melvin in a convalescent home, he brags about the whippings he got as a boy, "with a bullwhip, a hickory whip, and even the hard root of a sugar cane stalk." He deserved it, jokes my grandmother. She used to sit in a rocking chair on her grandmother's porch under a chinaberry tree keeping a lookout on her bad cousins. Melvin once dumped sand in the water well. Another time he put a cat in the oven and cooked it. He even wove cotton between a sleeping relative's toes and set it on fire. During our visit, Melvin claims that he used to pick three hundred pounds of cotton a day. No one believes him but we go along with the tall tale anyway.

Next to Old Morning Star Church is Buie's Grocery Store, still owned by Lenon Buie. In back is a large garden with long rows of bell peppers, tomatoes, mustard, collard and turnip greens, yellow squash, peas, butter beans, cucumber, and okra. "I don't bother with watermelon anymore," he tells us. I wander through the garden with Laura, who works in a hospital and owns a three-bedroom home in the city, as we try to figure out which green leaves are squash and which okra. I love the feel of the soil in my hands. Always have. I get that from my father, who is a gardener and landscaper. It's in my blood.

My grandmother, who is eighty-three and returning here for the first time since 1930, has never had a garden that I know of. And this is my mother's first time ever seeing the South. The only reason my mother and grandmother (who raised me together, with my cousin Lisa in Los Angeles) are here now, is because I asked them to come.

Cousin Clem—who my grandmother still calls a "fine, young man"—shows us photocopies of U.S. Census Records that he has made in preparation for our visit, telling us all about "the white guy" (as my mother puts it) who was my great grandfather. We were enjoying lunch at the local Western Sizzlin' Restaurant. The buffet menu included sweet potatoes, collard greens, macaroni and cheese, ribs, and fried chicken. The décor was modest, but the food was home-style good.

"We couldn't have even gone into a restaurant like this when I was a girl," my grandmother reminds me. I take it for granted that we can go anywhere we want. This sense of privilege is magnified in me, in part, because of my light skin and the fact that my father is white. When I was here, my grandmother continues, "grown men had to say 'sir' to little white boys. They lived through all that," she adds, her voice becoming indignant.

I know even as I write these words that I am romanticizing a way of life that was not in the least bit romantic. And yet, I can't help wishing that more black girls and boys sat on their family's porches at dusk, watching the sun go down and shelling purple hull peas for dinner.

* * *

As I finish the final chapters of this book, my television

remains tuned 24-7 to CNN so that I can monitor the devastating impact of our government's neglect of black people and poor whites in the wake of Hurricane Katrina. Over 100 volunteer surgeons are stranded in Mississippi for more than thirty hours, unable to reach survivors. A shelter is closed after residents drink contaminated water and develop dysentery. A mobile hospital with 113 beds remains parked 70 miles north of New Orleans for days, waiting for red tape to let it through, while the sick and elderly die like animals in the streets. Hundreds of children are missing and CNN is doing a better job of finding them than the Feds, while Wal-Mart, of all people, was one of the first to arrive with water, long before the people we pay to handle emergencies. It is an outrage and I wish I were there to bear witness. It is our job, as journalists, at least to do that.

But this is nothing new. During the Mississippi flood of 1927, as notes author Pete Daniel among others, poor blacks were the ones who suffered most, making up nearly half of the 770,000 displaced residents. White women and children were evacuated by boat while African Americans were stranded for days without food or water. And it got worse. I have an old videotape somewhere, documentary footage that shows how black people trying to head north after losing their homes and livelihoods found themselves suddenly arrested for "vagrancy" and put to work—forced labor at gunpoint—

along the Mississippi River packing sand bags. Herbert Hoover attempted to keep such reports out of the media.

Now, here we are again, full circle as the entire city of New Orleans, where 67 percent of residents are African American and mostly poor, was left to die like dogs along the side of the road. None of this surprises Sarah White. "We always been last on everything and probably always will," she says when I reach her by phone a few days after the hurricane. "This here storm just tops it off," she adds. "The entire justice system and the people who run it just showed us that we aren't important."

But we must be important to ourselves, if to no one else.

* * *

The Taheebo tree is found in the jungles of the South American Amazon. It yields brilliant magenta-pink flowers. Its inner bark is a liver booster, fever-reducer, anti-inflammatory agent, and hormone balancer called *pau d'arco*. The herb is widely prescribed for cancer patients throughout Brazil, Argentina, and Peru. Also known as *lapacho*, it is said to heal ulcers, as well as viral and autoimmune disorders ranging from herpes to lupus. And, yet, as Daniel B. Mowrey, Ph.D., author of *Herbal Tonic Therapies* writes, the American medical establishment is only interested in discovering a single, patented ingredient that can be bought and sold for profit. The problem is that "no isolated component of lapacho comes anywhere close to being equal to the combined activity of the whole herb."

Dandelion, too, which the old Southern black women drank as tea for depression contains carotenoids, choline, inulin, pectin, potash, bitter substances, phytosterols, sugars and triterpenes—nothing particularly magical on its own. And, yet, through a complex interaction these ingredients work *together* to heal everything from liver and gall bladder problems to hormonal disorders and diabetes. The real magic, says Mowrey, "*is in the incredible synergy that exists among the constituent parts.*"

In the movie *Love & Basketball*, one of my favorite scenes is when Monica's mother (Alfre Woodard) musters up all her "ladylike" etiquette and courage to give one final piece of advice. "I've always admired the fight in you," she confesses to her daughter. Even though I never learned how to do it for myself, she tells Monica, bringing tears to my eyes every time I watch, *I can still teach you.*

Fight for your life, she tells her daughter.

Each of the women in this book has taught me so much. Their stories have urged me forward, propelling me to outrage and action. And they have settled and calmed me too, reminding me how to nurture and receive love. On each of our collective and individual journeys toward power, I believe that we need only look to each other to find the missing, hurt, and neglected parts of ourselves. The past repeats; shared history and bloodlines endure. And we remain: each of us, still, connected.